# Cook It Raw

# Cook It Raw

Edited by Alessandro Porcelli

# Contents

'Fifteen chefs go out for a walk in the forest ...' It sounds like the beginning of a joke – or a slasher film. But that's more or less what Cook It Raw has been making happen: it plucks the very best and most forward-thinking chefs in the world from their kitchens, their 'laboratoires', their 'ateliers', and deposits them as far as can be imagined from their usual comfort zones, leaving them to forage for ingredients in the Collio hills along the Italian-Slovenian border, fish for a main course in Lapland, or wade upstream in search of wild wasabi in Ishikawa prefecture in Japan.

The selection process for invitees each year is mysterious – though it is clearly an honour to be asked. When invited to do anything in the company of internationally recognized innovators like Albert Adrià, David Chang, René Redzepi, Massimo Bottura and Alex Atala, few would not leap at the chance.

But Cook It Raw is not a food and wine festival. Participants will presumably, at some point, 'cook' food. And (chefs being chefs) there will surely be wine. But there are no tickets sold. No tasting tents, co-branded cooking demonstrations, sponsored parties – the usual razzmatazz of events that, to these chefs, have become part of a day's work. At Cook It Raw, chefs are invited somewhere new each year to learn, to explore, to exchange ideas. And, most interestingly, to fail, gloriously, by creating dishes they have never attempted before.

They are invited to learn something new about an unfamiliar place, make maximum use of its local ingredients, take note of traditional preparation methods, and then – in full view of the very best of their peers – do the most spectacularly fucked-up thing they can imagine, with whatever they've found.

One doesn't arrive at Cook It Raw prepared to crank out some battle-tested signature dish that long experience has taught is perfect for the venue. The challenge is to do what has never been done before – by anyone. This is exactly the opposite of what every other gathering of chefs expects. Perhaps the greatest difference between the conventional model of the food 'event' and this mutant roadshow is that there is no 'audience' in the usual sense. At the climax of a few days of experimentation, planning, hunting, foraging, gathering (and heavy drinking), the chefs convene to cook for a very few select journalists and local purveyors, craftsmen and dignitaries. These, however, are not really the intended end user. There is no judging, after-action report or measure of a particular dish's success or failure. What the chefs are actually doing is cooking for each other.

The restaurant business demands repetition — at its very core, it insists that a customer who enjoys a dish one day should be able to return a week later with friends and receive exactly the same thing. In the best case scenario, that dish will become much loved, widely written about, frequently imitated — a signature dish. This would be the very definition, by traditional restaurant metrics, of 'success'.

But a signature dish is also a prison. One cannot remove it from a menu. Two signature dishes are two slots on a menu where the chef can no longer be creative but only repeat what he has done before. To travel to the other side of the world, then, and be invited to fail — and not just fail but fail spectacularly — all in the name of unfettered creativity? That is truly a wonderful thing.

For centuries a principal engine of gastronomy has been trial and error, yet the business of keeping a restaurant's doors open — especially in a shrinking economy — makes such things difficult and often impossible. Pure innovation for its own sake — the imagination run wild — is what elevates the profession, lifts food from necessity to pleasure, from sustenance to a craft and, in very rare cases, to art.

Cook It Raw, among other missions, intends nothing less than that.

## The birth of Raw – by Alessandro Porcelli

Half serious culinary conference, half major blowout, chefs congresses have established themselves as important dates in the gastronomic calendar since their inception in the late nineties. The first congress – at least in the format that they exist in now – started in San Sebastian, northeastern Spain. They developed as a means of showcasing the techno-emotional culinary revolution that was sweeping through Spain at the time. This revolution was big, but in my mind, the great shift in kitchen culture they marked, was bigger.

Throughout most of restaurant history kitchens were like castles. They stood alone, closed and impenetrable, a safe for holding secret signature dishes and techniques. Chefs did not share, they did not care about one another; the success of a peer was a source of jealousy, not joy. What these congresses did was blow open the gates of such strongholds. They encouraged chefs to talk, to share, to show each other how to improve. They gave birth to a new culture of openness.

I vividly recall the first food conference that I ever attended – Omnivore, in Northern France, in the mid 2000's. The event was dedicated to 'young cuisine' and its organisers scoured the gastronomic map to find the freshest talent to demonstrate what they were about. That year, it was the turn of René Redzepi from restaurant Noma in Copenhagen.

At that time, I was working at Noma and, as the restaurant's resident extrovert, René decided that I might be an interesting – or at least, entertaining – travelling partner. I am forever glad he thought so, because attending that event simply blew my mind. It was like nothing I had ever experienced and, although I couldn't know it then, would subsequently change the course of my life.

After Omnivore, I was keen to see what other conferences were like and the timing was perfect. Noma was beginning to establish itself on the culinary scene and René was being invited to every major food event. I was fortunate enough to be able to join him at the likes of Lo Mejo de la Gastronomia, Madrid Fusion and Milan's Identita Golose.

Unfortunately, the following few years saw the conferences change dramatically. Good things rarely last. The huge crowds they had begun to attract had turned them into circuses, not to mention huge money-spinners. Auditoriums were plastered with sponsorship and events branded within an inch of their lives. Not surprisingly the connection between the chefs was affected and a big gulf opened up between them and the audience. For many of us, the chefs' congress was a victim of its own success and it all felt very wrong.

Yet there was still hope. Off stage, after the demos – in the restaurants and bars of whichever town happened to be hosting that event – the scene was entirely different. Chefs would get together. They'd eat, drink, talk and forge friendships. This was what they looked forward to most at the conferences – this was why they had come.

In 2006, at the end of another Omnivore edition, Andrea Petrini – then (and now) the industry's most well-connected journalist, asked a group of some of the chummiest chefs, to take part in Gelinaz – a sort of improv-theatre-meets-fine-dining event. A culinary jam session. The idea was to take a single dish – this time one of Davide Scabin's – and have the chefs each create their own interpretation of it.

I was lucky enough to attend the gig. Watching the chefs work together, tasting and commenting on one another's food, was like nothing I'd seen at any of the conferences. Free from the restrictive demonstration format, the chefs seemed genuinely inspired and happy. I made a mental note of the set-up, not really knowing what I might do with it.

Meanwhile, at Noma, things were going from good to better and from better to great. All of René's hard work in creating the restaurant was finally starting to pay off. Restaurant magazine named Noma thirty-third best in the world and almost overnight, the restaurant went from being rarely fully booked to having a huge waiting list. But while much of the world's press were keen to find out about 'new Nordic cuisine', there were plenty within the trade that remained suspicious and skeptical. At conferences they'd tease, 'You're from Denmark … isn't Danish food just frozen peas?' A combination of Rene's Danish pride and my lasting excitement about what I'd seen at Gelinaz made us determined to prove them all wrong. We decided an event was the best way to do it and began planning it.

In 2007, we invited fifteen chefs to Noma to cook using only Nordic ingredients. We called the event Looking North. Andrea Petrini, who'd since become a big champion of René's and a Noma regular, opened his address book and used his considerable charm to help us convince Alain Passard, Carlo Cracco, Massimo Bottura, Wylie Dufresne, Petter Nilsson, Iñaki Aizpitarte and many more of the hottest chefs of the moment to accept the invitation. Looking North concluded with another installment of Gelinaz. It left the chefs and attending journalists in little doubt that Danish food was a force to be reckoned with, while I felt even more convinced that there was real potential in a more free-form chef's gathering.

Looking North marked my last day working at Noma. I left to set up my own company, Nordic Gourmet Tour. My intention was to capitalise on the increasing interest in Danish food by organising gastronomic tours of the country. Business was disappointingly slow so

I busied myself pitching culinary event after culinary event to the Danish tourist board.

Eventually, in the summer of 2008, they bit and I organized an event that ran alongside the tourist board's own Copenhagen Cooking food festival. Aimed at bringing Danish gastronomy down to eye level, I invited the country's top chefs to cook for the public. The crowds exceeded everyone's expectations and I was thrilled Andrea was there to capture it all for Gambero Rosso TV.

Shortly after, I began consulting for the Danish government. The government were still reeling from the fallout of the scandal surrounding the Jyllands-Posten's Prophet Mohammed cartoons and were desperate for some positive PR. Food, they'd decided was the way forward. With the United Nations Climate Change Conference in Copenhagen coming up, I made the suggestion that they stage a gastronomic event with an environmental agenda. They gave me the green light and I immediately put a call in to René and Andrea to ask for their help.

Creating an event relevant to the Climate Conference was easy. René's brand of New Nordic cuisine, with its emphasis on local and seasonal produce, foraged or grown in totally sustainable ways, was undeniably eco. The hard part, the part that I struggled with, was what to call the project and what format to give it. By this point, I had plenty of experience with chef events but with the world looking on I felt pressure to bring something new to the table.

After weeks of deliberation, I awoke one afternoon from a short nap with the answer: Cook It Raw. We would strip the chefs and the gastronomy that they practised right back to basics. We'd ask them to leave their tools, intricate techniques and expensive ingredients at home. We would give them an issue to contend with – in this case a future where energy was limited. We'd throw them into the natural world to contemplate it and then ask them to serve their answer up on a plate.

We invited a dozen of the most influential and creative young chefs in the world to the first edition of Cook It Raw in Copenhagen and have done to every one since. The roster changes, but regular participants include René Redzepi (Noma); Albert Adrià (Tickets; 41°); Iñaki Aizpitarte (Le Chateaubriand); David Chang (Momofuku); Massimo Bottura (Osteria Francescana); Ben Shewry (Attica); Alex Atala (D.O.M); Davide Scabin (Combal Zero); Claude Bosi (Hibiscus); Daniel Patterson (Coi); Pascal Barbot (L'Astrance); Magnus Nilsson (Fäviken); Petter Nilsson (La Gazzetta) and Yoshihiro Narisawa (Les Créations de Narisawa). The group is united not by their fame but by their willingness to use food as a vehicle for learning, exploration and change.

All of the above chefs would agree that they are only ever as good as their ingredients thus local producers have become an integral part of the Cook It Raw experience. We started by meeting the farmer Søren Wiuff in Copenhagen and have since gone on to meet incredible wine producers (Josko Gravner and Marco Perco), hunters (Jarkko Kuusisto), farmers (Yoshihiro Yokomichi) and artisans (Utatsuyama Craft School).

Using food to explore issues is integral to the philosophy of Cook It Raw and each new edition poses a different question, against a different geographical background. Across several days the chefs immerse themselves in the question and the place. They fish, hunt, forage and engage with local people and traditions before presenting their conclusions in culinary form at a dinner for special guests and journalists. Cook It Raw doesn't end, however, when the last dish is served and the chefs go home. By bringing their own creativity and unique perspective to traditional products and practices, the chefs can help re-invigorate local food culture. What's more, often the chefs themselves have been changed and the new things they have seen, experienced and tasted serve as sources of inspiration in their own kitchens.

Four events and four questions later and Cook It Raw still holds on to this basic format. In the pages that follow, you'll read and see just how surprisingly fitting the term 'Raw' turned out to be, as the chefs involved are undeniably original and incredibly intense and the experience itself is often rough, unrefined and occasionally painful. In spite of this, or maybe because of it, Cook It Raw is a phenomenally authentic chefs event and that's genuinely all that I ever really hoped to create.

Running his fingers through the grass, the planet's most famous forager turned to the superstar chef from Manhattan. 'If there's chicken shit on it, don't pick it,' he said. As the two knelt together on a hillock in a forgotten region of Italy they looked more like boy scouts on a camping trip than world-renowned chefs. It was not the most glamorous way to spend a Saturday morning, and would bring them neither pay nor glory. So what was it that inspired these incredibly busy men and several more like them to get on a plane and head out into the wilderness together?

A collaborative group of international top-notch chefs is an exceptional concept. Cooking has always been something of a competitive, sport. In fact, the notion of sharing ideas only started to catch on at the turn of the millennium with the advent of chefs' congresses. And yet these weren't really social gatherings. Participants had little time to hang out together.

In 2005, the food writer Andrea Petrini co-founded a chefs' collective called Gelinaz! The group got together four times in the next two years and included several future members of Cook It Raw: Massimo Bottura, Iñaki Aizpitarte, Rene Redzepi, Petter Nilsson and Davide Scabin. Taking the notion of sharing culinary ideas one step further, each riffed on a single dish to come up with his own version.

When Petrini joined Alessandro Porcelli a few years later to plan the first Cook It Raw event, his thoughts turned to the members of Gelinaz! 'They had compatible cooking styles: mostly vegetables, very experimental, open to improvisation,' he explained. More important, they had become friends.

Or rather, buddies. Each Cook It Raw event is like a reunion tour, complete with bear hugs, good-natured teasing and late nights drinking heavily while talking about – what else? – food.

These guys are undeniably food-obsessed, to the point that at least one of them has vegetables tattooed on his skin. But they are also curious about the world beyond the stoves. Back home, Daniel Patterson plays keyboards in a Syd Barrett tribute band while Massimo Bottura collects contemporary art and Alex Atala buys fair trade food products from Amazonian tribes in an effort to improve their living conditions.

Several cross their love of food with the inquisitiveness of a mad scientist, conducting experiments in their own laboratories or collaborating with university researchers. Back in 1997, Adrià started running elBulli's Taller, developing new culinary forms such as spherified cantaloupe and microwave sponge cake. Redzepi oversees the Nordic Food Lab, a non-profit organization dedicated to edible science projects including fermented crickets.

Cook It Raw imposes its own uncontrolled variables, from strange products to less-than-ideal conditions. These chefs get an obvious rush from the creative challenges. But it can be a major source of stress, too. Adrià admits he won't sleep for a week if his dish is a failure. 'It's not easy to improvise with products you don't normally use, or that aren't at all familiar,' he says.

At one time or another, Claude Bosi's pig blood went missing, Patterson's beets wouldn't cook fast enough, the freezer holding Redzepi's ice cream switched to defrost, and the Japanese duck hunt meant to provide Sean Brock's main ingredient turned up not a single bird. But the pressure also brings them closer, as they help each other out of rough spots.

'I think there is a spiritual thing that brings us together,' says Redzepi. 'Nobody is pretentious. People are quite open – they don't feel they've finished learning. None of these guys see themselves as artists.' That is rare at this level – which is to say, the top. In the years since Cook It Raw began, its participants have watched each other grow and become increasingly successful. Now, it is as though the top seeds in tennis had gathered just to work on their strokes together. No matter how busy they are, most of these chefs wouldn't miss it for the world. The three-star chef Pascal Barbot cooked Friday night dinner at his restaurant in Paris, then travelled for 17 hours to join the others for an abbreviated weekend in Lapland.

Cook It Raw exemplifies what has been called the 'Supernatural' culinary movement – stepping out into the wild and creating food defined by a specific time and place. This new generation of chefs are tuned into their environment, in every sense of the word. Many of them feel a responsibility to the earth and its bounty, are aware of their influence and consider themselves role models.

Beyond the partying, Cook It Raw also embodies the brutality of the life cycle. And as this band of chefs forage, hunt and cook together like the boys in Lord of the Flies, some of the most unforgettable gastronomic experiences they create are the darkest and most disturbing. The acrid taste of blood from a freshly slaughtered pig; a beloved ox boiled down to its essence and smeared on to the sides of champagne glasses; fjord shrimp so alive they are literally jumping until that life is extinguished by the crunch of human teeth.

'Raw' fits into the zeitgeist, that you want to understand the beginning of everything, and be connected to that again,' says Redzepi. 'Essential ideas like life and death. What you put in your mouth, it becomes a part of you.' Eating is a carnal, primitive act: the transfer of matter and energy from one being to another. But while food provides sustenance, cooking can be the foundation of true camaraderie.

Albert Adrià

Iñaki Aizpitarte

On a grey day in March 1985 Albert Adrià, aged fifteen, dropped out of school and left home to join his brother Ferran in the kitchen at elBulli, on Spain's Costa Brava. Ferran had only been there a year, and the restaurant was not yet the temple of groundbreaking gastronomy it would soon become. Albert remained at elBulli for twenty-three years, taking charge of pastries in 1987, and then heading up the workshop where culinary experiments were run. He and his brother became leaders of the molecular trend by pioneering techniques from foam to spherification. At Ferran's side, Albert helped turn elBulli into the most famous restaurant on the planet, and Spain into its culinary mecca. With his extraordinary re-creations of nature, he earned a reputation as the most imaginative pastry chef of his generation. But it's not easy working for the world's best-known restaurant, or for an older sibling. It's only since leaving elBulli that Albert has really come into his own, as an equal partner with his brother in a number of wildly successful ventures in Barcelona, including Tickets, a circus-like tapas bar, and 41° Experience, a cocktail bar with music, lights and the fireworks of their cuisine.

Never quite where you expect him to be, Aizpitarte grew up in France but discovered cooking in Israel. He comes across as lackadaisical, yet created the buzziest bistro in Paris. Then this renegade chef bagged one of the most prestigious distinctions in France, the Chevalier de l'Ordre des Arts et des Lettres. The eye-pleasing, notoriously unpredictable Basque chef was born (the youngest of five) to a French family of modest means. Rather than attend university, he drifted from job to job. In his late twenties he went to Tel Aviv and fell into the restaurant business, working first as a dishwasher, then as a cook. When he returned to Paris via Latin America he continued learning in various kitchens before opening his own bare-bones bistro, Le Châteaubriand, followed a few years later by Le Dauphin, a Rem Koolhaas-designed French tapas bar. A marvellously instinctive chef, Aizpitarte creates simple, finely executed dishes marrying strong flavours in unlikely combinations such as mackerel with lychees, or red berry piperade. His food is often stunningly good and invariably as hard to predict as his personality.

Fredrik Andersson

Alex Atala

With his puckish features and goat-like beard, Fredrik Andersson looks like someone you might find on a mountaintop. Fortunately, you can track him down at ground level in Enskededalen, a leafy suburb of Stockholm. This is where he and his partner moved their restaurant, Mistral, a few years ago in order to be closer to the source of their biodynamic products. (While in central Stockholm, they had had a Michelin star.) Andersson builds his menus from the best-quality local seasonal ingredients, furnished by three nearby farms and the woods where he forages for herbs and flowers, wild fish, game and birds. His minimalist and vegetable-driven cooking reflects the current Nordic sensibility, while the unforgiving local climate only serves to stimulate his creativity.

Though raised a city boy in São Bernardo do Campo, Alex Atala often went with his father to fish for dinner in the ocean and pick fruit in the Brazilian rainforest. He has always been, as he says, an 'independent personality', and at fourteen he left home for good to join São Paolo's rock and roll scene. After working as a DJ he took off once again, backpacking through Europe. In Belgium he enrolled in catering school purely to get a visa, and there he discovered his calling as a chef. Atala perfected his skills in some of Europe's top kitchens before returning to São Paulo and opening a gastronomic table named D.O.M. At D.O.M. he applies haute cuisine techniques to indigenous products such the enormous freshwater fish known as pirarucu.

On the surface, Atala seems to be pure testosterone. Yet, there's a caring nature beneath the he-man physique: he once acquired 57,000 acres of rainforest in order to protect it, and he researches sustainable new food products for the benefit of Amazonian tribes. Priprioca, for example, is a fragrant root normally used in cosmetics; Atala pairs it with chocolate cream.

14

Pascal Barbot

Mark Best

In the minuscule kitchen of his small Paris restaurant, Pascal Barbot uses his remarkably precise hands to create exquisite food. Growing up in the Auvergne, he had always wanted to become a chef. After perfecting his skills with Alain Passard, he and a colleague opened L'Astrance in 2000. In short order they racked up three Michelin stars. This was despite the fact that the restaurant has only twenty-five covers, is closed at weekends, and offers a no-choice menu based on what the chef finds at the market. Barbot has never let success go to his head and, unlike many chefs of his standing, he shows up at the restaurant for every single shift. Potential diners, on the other hand, don't get through the door so easily, as a table at L'Astrance is one of the city's most coveted reservations. Those who succeed are rewarded by a cooking style that is contemporary and curious, infused with flavours from Barbot's many travels abroad. His favourite tool is a mortar and pestle from Thailand. And his signature dish is a galette of foie gras marinated in verjus, then layered with paper-thin slices of raw white mushroom – a simple, perfectly balanced combination of the humble and refined.

Mark's road to recognition as one of Australia's best chefs was an indirect one: he worked as an electrician in gold mines until, at the age of twenty-five, he decided to apprentice in a bistro kitchen (and took a major pay cut in the process). After eating at L'Arpège in Paris he knew that was where he must train, and did so for four months, learning the perfection of French technique and an aversion to complacency. In 1999, he and his wife opened the fifty-cover Marque in Sydney. A guy who can work 4,000 feet (1,300 metres) underground is not one to shy away from risk, and Best's kitchen challenges his customers with bold creations such as raw tuna on a brioche with foie gras custard and pork crackling. His food is electric.

Claude Bosi

Massimo Bottura

Claude Bosi grew up in Lyon in eastern France, where his parents ran a bistro. A wild child, he once accidentally set fire to the kitchen while frying an egg. And when he was fourteen the school authorities told his parents that although his work was good they didn't want him around any more. 'I decided then and there to become a cook,' he recalls. For the next year he 'pre-apprenticed' at a friend's brasserie, full-time and without pay. That led to an apprenticeship with Jean-Paul Lacombe and later stints with Alain Passard and Alain Ducasse. He moved to Ludlow in England to improve his language skills while working as a sous-chef. With his then wife, Claire, he finally opened his own restaurant, Hibiscus, and earned two Michelin stars. In 2007 the couple relocated Hibiscus from Ludlow to London, quickly regaining their stars. The majority of Bosi's raw materials come from Britain's small farms and producers, and are always seasonal ones. His cuisine is modern and surprising, the flavours of each ingredient dialled up to maximum, such as roasted scallops with pork pie sauce and pink grapefruit puree. Some critics describe his food as feminine, despite the lamb testicles that often appear on the menu.

Born to a well-off family in Modena, Bottura started out working in the family's heating oil business. His passion, however, was food, and at twenty-three he bought a trattoria and turned it into a popular local dining spot. One day Alain Ducasse dined there and invited Bottura to come and be an apprentice at the Hôtel de Paris. Massimo accepted, and in 1994 sold the trattoria. He also spent time at elBulli, learning about sous-vide and dehydration, but mostly how to experiment with food. When Bottura opened Osteria Francescana in his home town in 1995, his cutting-edge cuisine shocked traditionalists. In fact, he had such a hard time that he nearly shut it down. Fortunately, he hung on, eventually earning three Michelin stars and fourth place on the World's 50 Best Restaurants list. Ingredients of the highest quality possible are key to his cuisine. Not only does he produce his own balsamic vinegar, he also helped to save the Bianca Val Padana breed of cattle from extinction. Their milk makes the world's best Parmesan, and has done so since the Middle Ages. But when Bottura deconstructs the cheese into foam and air, it is anything but medieval.

Sean Brock

David Chang

Brock grew up shucking corn in a tiny coal-mining town in West Virginia. Today he has a cob of very rare corn tattooed on his arm and runs a restaurant named Husk (along with another, McCrady's) in Charleston, South Carolina. Working with historians and plant geneticists, Brock has given new life to heirloom grains and vegetables from the pre-Civil War South. Embracing both traditional and twenty-first-century cooking methods, from barbecue to sous-vide, he works wonders with fresh, locally grown products. In doing so, he has opened people's eyes to Southern American cooking beyond the stereotypical fried chicken and grits. Brock won the James Beard Best Chef Southeast award in 2010; a year later Bon Appétit magazine named Husk 'The Best New Restaurant in America'.

New York City has not been the same since David Chang came to town and opened his hole-in-the-wall ramen joint in the East Village in 2004. At first utterly ignored and then endlessly imitated, the Momofuku Noodle Bar ultimately turned Chang into a superstar. When his parents emigrated from Korea in the 1960s his father demonstrated the ambitious streak that would reappear in his son, starting out as a dishwasher in New York City and eventually running a golf supplies business outside Washington, D.C. This is where David grew up, eating his mother's Korean barbecue and kimchi. After college he moved to Japan, an experience that taught him restaurant food didn't have to be expensive to be delicious. Chang's vision mixes his Asian roots with European technique and the best of American food culture. Thanks to him, New Yorkers have developed an addiction to fluffy pork buns, among other delights. He now runs a restaurant group that extends from Manhattan via Sydney to Toronto, and his impact stretches further – a quarterly food journal (Lucky Peach), a role on a TV series (Treme), even a place on Time magazine's 100 list as one of the most influential people of 2010.

Mauro Colagreco

Quique Dacosta

He may be a foreigner on French soil, but Mauro Colagreco has quickly won over fussy Gallic palates. Michelin awarded him a star ten months after he opened his restaurant on the Riviera, followed with a second one five years later. When the Gault-Millau guide named him Chef of the Year, he became the first non-native to receive this honour. Born in Argentina to parents of Spanish and Italian ancestry, Mauro moved to France to work with Bernard Loiseau and then as Alain Passard's second-in-command. In 2006, he took over the Mirazur, just a few steps from the Italian border with a drop-dead view of the Mediterranean. The restaurant has two gardens of its own – one for herbs and citrus fruit, another for vegetables and forty varieties of tomatoes. Colagreco's vibrant cooking deftly mixes this home-grown produce with ingredients from the land and sea, such as oysters wrapped in pear carpaccio with shallot cream, or briefly cooked langoustines (Norweigan lobster) with flowers. If you could eat the Côte d'Azur, this is how it would taste.

It was during a spell as a dishwasher at the age of fourteen that Quique Dacosta discovered a love for the restaurant business. He has come a long way since then, and now runs his own two-Michelin-star temple to Spanish avant-garde cuisine. His creative development coincided with the blossoming of Spain as ground zero for Modernist cooking, and since the closing of elBulli he has been considered one of the movement's leading lights. Located in the tourist town of Denia, on the Costa Blanca, Dacosta's eponymous restaurant makes the most of his region's products - Senia rice, blood oranges, and fabulous seafood including sweet red prawns (shrimp). The chef also creates magic through molecular transformations, such as gelatine 'eggs' or peppers made from watermelon. Just as elBulli did, his restaurant closes for several months each year to allow the team time to develop new dishes and stay one step ahead.

Alexandre Gauthier

Ichiro Kubota

The year 1979 brought two happy additions to the Gauthier family. In March, Roland Gauthier acquired a traditional French restaurant called L'Auberge de la Grenouillère (the Frog Pond Inn) in the northern Pas-de-Calais region. Two months later, his son Alexandre was born. The younger Gauthier eventually followed in his father's footsteps, first training at cookery school and then doing apprenticeships with the likes of Régis Marcon and Michel Roth. In 2001 the Grenouillère lost its long-cherished Michelin star, but two years later Alexandre took over the restaurant. A new generation meant a brand-new style: out with the crêpes suzette, in with briefly cooked pigeon, lobster smoked over juniper branches and wild herbs. Pepper is the only spice he uses. Michelin took note of his straightforward, daring cuisine and in 2008 gave the restaurant its star back. In 2012, the World's 50 Best Restaurants awards named Gauthier 'one to watch'. This is one frog pond worth leaping into.

This Japanese chef thanks his father, a top Kyoto chef whom he calls his master, for instilling culinary values into him – though he didn't always listen. 'My father said, 'Never eat a hamburger. Your palate will be destroyed', he recalls. 'When I finished elementary school I invited my brother, nicked some money from my mother's purse, and we went to McDonald's. It was amazing.' Fortunately, Ichiro's palate survived the assault, and he went on to work in some of Kyoto's best kaiseki restaurants before leaving for France, where the restaurateur Marlon Abela discovered him and he was hired to head up the kitchen at his new London venture, Umu. Opened in 2004, it was the city's first Kyoto-style table. To make it authentic, Kubota flew in wild fish and vegetables from Japan, and imported water from the island of Kyushu. He picked up a Michelin star after only five months.

Yoshihiro Narisawa

Magnus Nilsson

Narisawa's grandfather ran a Japanese sweet shop, his father a Western-style one, and his own culinary style is a hybrid of the two cultures. He had always wanted to be a chef, and at nineteen left Japan to train in Switzerland, France and Italy under greats such as Frédy Girardet and Joël Robuchon. Today Narisawa runs an eponymous twenty-five seat table in Tokyo that has risen as high as number twelve on the World's 50 Best Restaurants list. He applies his hard-earned European techniques – from classic French to molecular – to the Japanese concept of shun, the precise moment when ingredients are at their peak. Narisawa's beautiful culinary compositions bear evocative names such as 'Soil Soup' or 'Landscape of February', with green buds pushing through grated turnips representing snow. Made of ingredients such as twigs and berries, wild hare and ash from charred vegetables, the flavours are like a walk in the woods.

This chef looks like a babyfaced version of the Nordic thunder god Thor, but he has a poise and maturity beyond his years. He grew up on the Swedish island of Frösön, south of the Arctic Circle, and now runs the kitchen at Fäviken Magasinet, fify miles (eighty-five kilometres) away. In between, he sharpened his skills at L'Astrance in Paris, then left cooking for a while, feeling that he needed to discover a style of his own. Fortunately, he found it – what he calls 'rektún mat', or real food, inspired by ingredients from Fäviken's 24,000-acre estate and surrounding area. It's audacious fare made with the best available products (much of which he hunts, fishes and forages himself), prepared simply and with a creativity born from limitation. Wild trout roe in a crust of dried pig's blood; steak from a dairy milk cow; marrow freshly scooped from a bone sawn in two in the dining room, are but a few dishes served at the restaurant. As Nilsson explains, 'We push the product to what we think would be perfect. Some dishes stay on the menu for years, but we are continually developing them.' A true Viking quest.

Petter Nilsson

Daniel Patterson

Born in a seaside town in southern Sweden, Petter Nilsson has cooked his way through Malmö, Copenhagen, Bordeaux and Uzès in the south of France, where he developed a serious following at Les Trois Salons. Now he heads up the kitchen at La Gazzetta, a stylish bistro in eastern Paris with a no-choice prix-fixe that's one of the best deals in town. Nilsson's cooking is as zen as his character: spare, unfussy, with lots of vegetables and practically no cream or butter. The French tend to write about the malice (mischief) of his culinary style, a startling liaison of flavours and textures such as poached egg with bergamot or octopus with salicornia. There is a certain delicacy to both the man and his cuisine. Confronted with a pig slaughter at Cook It Raw in Italy, he opted to create a vegetarian wild boar tartare, or, as he put it, 'something more kind'.

One of the San Francisco Bay Area's most original chefs, Patterson has shaken up the narrow definition of Northern Californian cuisine with Coi, his small gastronomic table in North Beach. 'Coi' is an Old French word meaning 'tranquil', but though the chef himself comes across as mild-mannered he can be mercurial, as evidenced by the pull-no-punches food articles he has written for the New York Times. When he had more free time, before multiple restaurants and children, he used to play keyboards in a hard-rocking Syd Barrett tribute band. In the kitchen, Patterson uses local, sustainable products and an abundance of wild plants (he's been foraging for nearly two decades). And while he respects the exceptional quality of Californian ingredients he never allows them to suffocate his creativity. Dishes such as abalone with sprouts and flowers beautifully evoke the landscape and have earned Coi two Michelin stars. With two more restaurants in Oakland and a food lab in the works, Patterson's footprint on the Northern Califonian dining scene is steadily expanding.

René Redzepi

Davide Scabin

He has been called the world's best chef, but that's too simple a description. Redzepi's approach to food perfectly encapsulates a time and place, the plate as microcosmos, from ingredients and cooking methods to the way it is consumed. At his Copenhagen restaurant, Noma, diners harvest root vegetables from edible soil and rip through beef tartare with their fingers. Critics ridiculed him when he co-founded Noma on the principle that it would serve a contemporary, purely Nordic cuisine at a time when high gastronomy in Denmark meant French or Italian. He proved his detractors wrong, taking overlooked regional products and preparing them with a creativity that knew no limits. The result earned him top position in the World's 50 Best Restaurants awards several years in a row. He has done as much as anybody to turn foraging into a twenty-first century global trend. A boat near the restaurant houses his Nordic Food Lab, a centre for scientific research, where study projects include a re-examination of insects as food (live ants are served at Noma). Obviously, this chef has not finished revolutionizing the way we eat.

Scabin relishes his reputation as an iconoclast, but there is method to the apparent madness of this Italian provocateur. A truck-driver's son, he smokes like a barbecue, has a movie-star head of silver hair and a voice so deep it would give Barry White pause. He even inspired an Italian film, Tutte Le Donne Della Mia Vita (All the Women in My Life), a comedy about a famous and totally irresponsible chef. When he was growing up he planned to become a computer hacker or a thief, but his mother steered him towards a career in the kitchen. Since 2002 he has run Combal. Zero, the long, skinny restaurant at the contemporary Castello di Rivoli museum outside Turin, where he has achieved two Michelin stars. His take on cuisine is avant-garde and always changing — if there's one constant, it's in breaking the rules. Scabin prepares rabbit to taste like tuna, boils macaroni for fifty minutes to make an ethereal soufflé, crafts sushi from veal and foie gras. At the end of the evening the dining room fills with helium balloons as diners burst plastic bags in their mouths and a mix of Campari and soda shoots out. And there lies the fundamental appeal of his approach: food as una festa.

Ben Shewry

Yoji Tokuyoshi and Kondo Takahiko

Shewry's dishes overflow with memories, notably of his childhood years spent on a farm in New Zealand where his family grew food, foraged wild plants and ate seafood from the coast. By the age of five he knew that he would be a chef, and at ten he was doing a mini-apprenticeship in a restaurant kitchen. Today he is in Australia, head chef at Attica in the suburbs of Melbourne, where he has earned a top one hundred spot on the World's 50 Best Restaurants list several years in a row. Deeply knowledgeable and endlessly curious, Shewry makes thrilling use of the exotic range of products from this part of the world, such as snow crab prepared like a little pile of snow, or a potato cooked in 'the earth it was grown' – a nod to Maori cooking methods.

Two of the finest ingredients in Massimo Bottura's kitchen are these two young chefs from Japan. Tokuyoshi hails from a family of pharmacists but he preferred cooking, notably Italian food, and left Japan to do an apprenticeship in Umbria. When that ended he looked for another job but without success. Then he came across the Osteria Francescana in a restaurant guide. In short, he phoned, Bottura answered, and he was off to Modena. In the years since, Tokuyoshi has risen to become the restaurant's second-in-command. He is now considered one of the most promising up-and-coming chefs in Europe.

Kondo Takahiko was born in Tokyo and started doing restaurant work there at the age of eighteen. Like Tokuyoshi, he was crazy about Italian cuisine and went to cook in Tuscany, the Veneto and Milan before ending up in Modena. He ate lunch at the Osteria Francescana in 2005, falling in love with the food and the conceptualism behind it. In return, Bottura gave him a job. Takahiko became pastry chef in 2010, and has contributed to some of the restaurant's most inventive desserts, which include the quirkily named, 'Oops, I dropped the lemon tart'.

Hans Välimäki

Joachim Wissler

Acting as head judge on TV's Top Chef Suomi has made Hans Välimäki a star in his native Finland. He's been preparing for the role for most of his life, starting when he baked his own pulla (sweet bread), at the age of twelve. After attending cookery and pâtisserie schools in Finland he worked as an apprentice in Germany and Sweden, then took over Chez Dominique, a classic French establishment in central Helsinki, in 1998. Since then he has coaxed the kitchen ever northward, offering a modern take on Finnish cuisine – marinated herring, reindeer pudding, a 'snowball' filled with mint and berries – along with the odd French delicacy to achieve an eclectic synthesis of culinary cultures.

If Germany has become a must on the foodie's globetrotting tour it is largely thanks to Joachim Wissler, one of the protagonists of the so-called New German School. He picked up a third Michelin star in 2005 as head chef at the restaurant Vendôme, housed in a baroque castle in Cologne. The chef's refined rustic style covers the entire spectrum from traditional culinary technique to molecular artistry, and he has opened the cupboard to earthy, often forgotten ingredients such as calf's heart, roebuck and pork stomach. His combinations are strikingly innovative (octopus marshmallow, anyone?) and his dishes can be so complex and colourful that they resemble abstract paintings.

# Cook It Raw (I)

## THE DINNERS:

**[I]** Denmark
**NATURE**
Zero energy cooking

Cook It Raw's inaugural dinner in Copenhagen sees the chefs explore nature through a zero energy cooking challenge.

**[III]** Finland
**COLLABORATION**
Cooking in the wild

Cook It Raw heads into the Lappish wilds to test the strength of the brotherhood by holding a collaborative dinner.

**[II]** Italy
**CREATIVITY**
Chef versus winter

During the depths of a Collio winter Cook It Raw's chefs prepare dinner in an experiment of creativity.

**[IV]** Japan
**FUTURE**
Avant-garde meets tradition

The chefs meet the producers and crafts men of Ishikawa to create a Cook It Raw dinner that marries avant-garde cooking with tradition.

## THE PRINCIPLES:

[I] Nature rules
[II] Limitations boost creativity

[III] Collaboration not competition
[IV] Look back to look forward

## THE CHEFS:

| | | |
|---|---|---|
| Albert Adrià | ........... | ES |
| Iñaki Aizpitarte | ........... | FR |
| Alex Atala | ........... | BR |
| Fredrik Andersson | ........... | SE |
| Pascal Barbot | ........... | FR |
| Mark Best | ........... | AU |
| Claude Bosi | ........... | UK |
| Massimo Bottura | ........... | IT |
| Sean Brock | ........... | US |
| David Chang | ........... | US |
| Mauro Colagreco | ........... | AR |
| Quique Dacosta | ........... | ES |
| Alexandre Gauthier | ........... | FR |

| | | |
|---|---|---|
| Ichiro Kubota | ........... | JP |
| Yoshihiro Narisawa | ........... | JP |
| Magnus Nilsson | ........... | SE |
| Petter Nilsson | ........... | SE |
| Daniel Patterson | ........... | US |
| René Redzepi | ........... | DK |
| Davide Scabin | ........... | IT |
| Ben Shewry | ........... | XX |
| Kondo Takahiko | ........... | JP |
| Yoji Tokuyoshi | ........... | JP |
| Hans Välimäki | ........... | FI |
| Joachim Wissler | ........... | DE |

In response to the United Nations Climate Conference, Cook It Raw holds its inaugural gathering in Copenhagen to explore nature and its place in contemporary gastronomy. Ingredients are foraged in the grounds of Dragsholm Castle before the chefs are challenged to each create a dish for the event's closing dinner using zero energy.

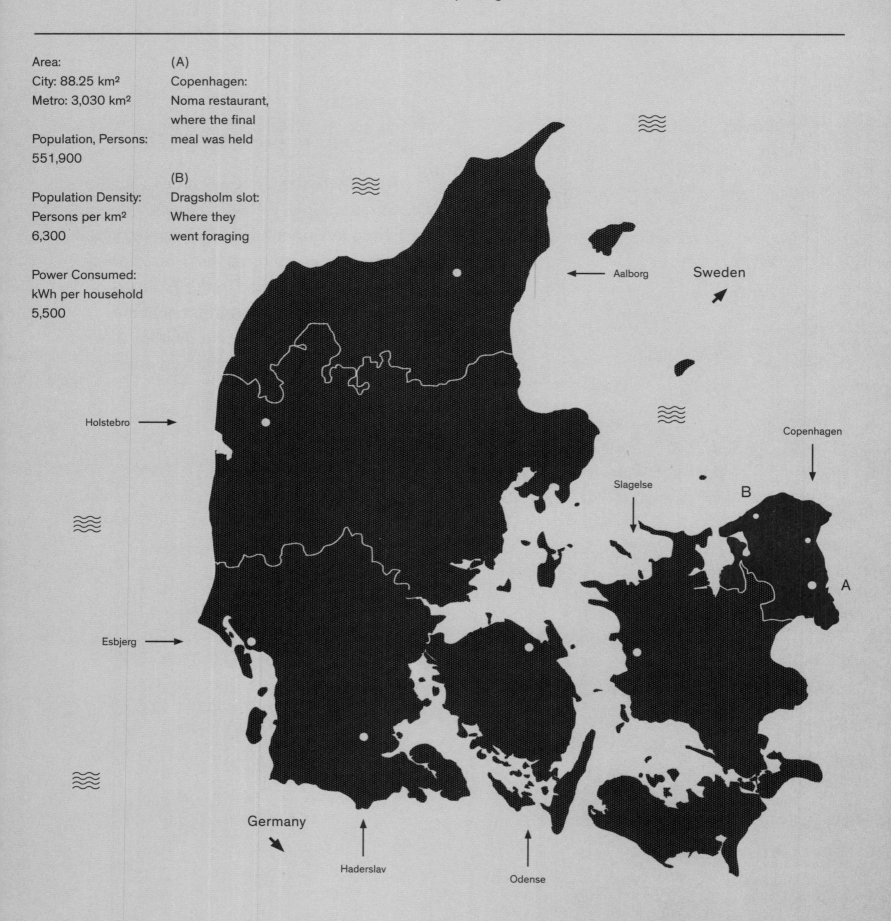

Area:
City: 88.25 km²
Metro: 3,030 km²

Population, Persons:
551,900

Population Density:
Persons per km²
6,300

Power Consumed:
kWh per household
5,500

(A)
Copenhagen:
Noma restaurant,
where the final
meal was held

(B)
Dragsholm slot:
Where they
went foraging

Aalborg

Sweden

Holstebro

Copenhagen

Slagelse

B

A

Esbjerg

Germany

Haderslav

Odense

## Raw Ingredients

The North West Zealand countryside is Cook It Raw's larder. In May the following ingredients are available to the chefs to forage:

| Meat: | Razor clams | Vegetables: |
|---|---|---|
| Pork | Large clams | Asparagus |
| Beef | Scallops | Beech leaf |
| Chicken | Medium size squid | Green strawberries |
| Venison | Lump fish roe | Sorrell |
| | Turbot | Hop shoots |
| Fish and Shellfish: | Cod | Chervil |
| Danish oysters | Sole | Lovage |
| Mussels | Monkfish | Horseradish |
| Small grey | Skate | Rhubarb |
| fjordshrimps | Herring | Radish |
| Sweet red shrimp | Pike perch | Woodruff |
| Langoustine | Grey mullet | Leeks |
| King crab | Eel | Cabbage |
| Normal crab | Salmon and | Beach coriander |
| Blue Danish lobster | smoked salmon | Wood peas |

## Sustainability Index
### (Copenhagen, 1990 = 100)

• • • Greenhouse gas emissions　——— Energy consumed　- - - Population

## Human Consumption of Food
### (Million kg)

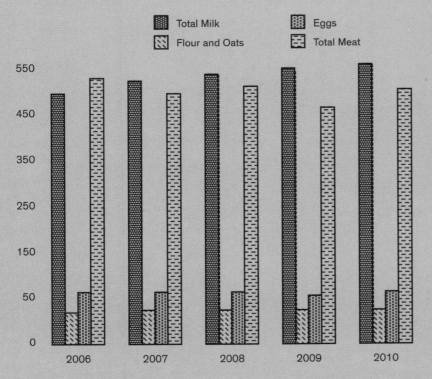

Legend:
- Total Milk
- Flour and Oats
- Eggs
- Total Meat

## Sustainable Cities

The top five most sustainable cities in the world are:

Copenhagen, Denmark
Vancouver, Canada
San Francisco, U.S.
Oslo, Norway
Curitiba, Brazil

As the most sustainable city in the world, Copenhagen was the natural choice of locations for the United Nations 2009 Climate Conference. Cook It Raw's chefs take their inspiration from the conference and the city that's on track to being the world's first $CO_2$ neutral capital.

I hate it when people compare food to sex. Mario Batali with his horndog line about the two things you put in someone? Gael Greene with her unsubtle innuendos about tongues and forks? The promiscuous use of 'orgasmic' as a culinary adjective and that winking insistence on 'food porn'? No thank you. It grosses me out, and not, as you might think, because of the bodily fluids.

My problem with the metaphor is how it is used. It tends to rest on a very goal-oriented, very American, very, shall we say, phallocentric view of both enterprises. Insert A into B and get C: pleasure. And honestly, who besides a 16-year-old boy wants to eat, or fuck, like that? Yet when Alessandro Porcelli asked me to write about the first edition of Cook It Raw, and told me to make it 'sexy,' I thought 'of course'.

Because imagine this: eleven young chefs at the height of their powers are boarding a bus that will take them to a dark forest, but they don't know that yet. Some have met each other before, some are even friends, and they all know of one another by reputation. But none is accustomed to prolonged intimacy with the colleagues he so admires. As a result, they are all a little tentative, as though they're on a blind date and going to a movie of which none of them has ever heard. A current of energy runs among them – the electricity of anticipation – filled with the promise of possible connection but tinged with doubt (even a bit of fear) about what comes next.

What else would you compare it to?

That's how the first Cook It Raw began, on a bright afternoon in May 2009. We had traveled from around the globe, these eleven chefs considered among the very best in the world, and twenty or so of the journalists responsible for that consideration. Back then none of us – not even the two men who organized the gathering – had any real sense of what Cook It Raw was, and certainly no idea of what it would become. And so, as we boarded the bus that first day, our conversations were stilted, even a little skeptical.

We drove for ninety minutes outside of town. When we disembarked, we were standing in front of a 800-year-old castle turned restaurant, where, after a brief tour, we were ushered outdoors toward a lunch of sausages and asparagus beer. Until this point it was, in other words, your average press trip. But when we were done eating, Petrini picked up a reed basket from a table covered with them, and made a joke about a gastronomic Blair Witch Project. Everyone laughed nervously. Porcelli pointed us toward the woods. And that's when things started to change.

29

The following night, the chefs would be cooking a private dinner at Noma, one course per chef. In addition to expressing his personal style, each was supposed to use his dish to reflect upon place, meaning this place: the forest at whose edge we were now standing, a few kilometers from the shore. There was one more thing. With COP 15 (the UN-sponsored meeting intended to forge a unified international response to climate change) scheduled to take place in Copenhagen a few months down the line, Porcelli and Petrini had added an environmental challenge to the task of making dinner. The chefs had to cook without using energy. That was the 'raw' in Cook It Raw.

Pressing his home court advantage, René Redzepi led the group towards a bog, and waded in. He pulled a knife from his pocket, reached below the water's surface, and extracted a plant nearly as tall as he. 'Hey guys,' he said in that earnestly enthusiastic way we would soon come to recognize. 'Try this.' It was a bulrush, the same as made up Moses' basket. After paring away the bulb, Redzepi offered bites to the other chefs, comparing its flavor to asparagus and cucumber. From the sidelines, Nadine Levy, Noma's reservations manager and René's wife, smiled resolutely. 'I can never go into the forest with him,' she whispered, 'because he's always putting things in his mouth.'

From the bog, René sent us into the forest with promises of wood sorrel and ramson. The sun cut through the trees, dappling the leaf-strewn ground with the kind of light you see in fairy tales. Claude Bosi was so taken by the experience that he turned to his cook and said, 'We're doing this when we get home.' Dave Chang – the fearsome Dave Chang who most of us knew then only for his outsized reputation – flipped his scarf over his shoulder, knelt, and daintily dropped elderflowers into his basket. He looked like a wood sprite.

From there we rode tractors to the beach. In the forest, the chefs had picked gently, tentatively, but now, with the wind whipping fiercely and Jørgen Stoltz, a ranger, explaining the bounty around them, they started harvesting in earnest. Greedily they passed each other tastes of sea buckthorn and wild mustard, and stuffed heaps of sweetarrow grass and purslane into plastic bags to take home. On the bus, beach coriander scented the air, but we still had one more stop to make. Søren Wiuff once grew a monoculture of carrots, but thanks to Redzepi's persuasive efforts, had diversified his crops so that he now cultivated the most wonderful array of vegetables, and had become one of Noma's primary suppliers. At his farm, we picked asparagus and sampled leeks left in the ground to winter. They were so crazy sweet that journalist Mattias Kroon called them dessert.

It's amazing what a day spent tromping through woods and sand will do for the appetites. When we met that night for dinner at Mads Reflund's restaurant in Copenhagen, any lingering social awkwardness had disappeared.

Everyone ate and drank ravenously and language barriers dissolved. Chang asked Iñaki Aizpitarte if he was a yeller in the kitchen. 'No', Aizpitarte replied, 'it's my staff that yells at me'. Eventually, the conversation turned, almost flirtatiously, to the following night's dinner. With the Talmudic dexterity of Bill Clinton, the chefs parsed the meaning of the word 'raw.' Albert Adrià, charged with the most difficult task – dessert – argued that forty seconds of microwaving didn't really count.

In the kitchen the next day, everyone was hungover, jet-lagged, nervous. Daniel Patterson worried that he had never seen half the herbs he had picked the day before. Massimo Bottura circulated photocopies of a newspaper article to make sure that everyone understood the premise of his dish: it was made of the only seafood – squid, monkfish, jellyfish, and algae – that scientists believed would be left once humankind destroyed the oceans. Pascal Barbot worked with intense concentration on his mackerel filets, talking to no one. Adrià muttered to himself about not being able to use any 'fucking heat' to caramelize the 'fucking elderflower sauce'.

Chefs are known for their egos, and kitchens are brutally hierarchical places, but the tension that day was less about rivalry than about the desperate desire not to fail in front of others you admire to the point of worship. Only Iñaki Aizpitarte seemed not to suffer from it; when Porcelli had called him weeks before and asked for his list of ingredients, Aizpitarte

had told him to get some squab liver. And lobster. And then abruptly hung up the phone. Everyone was mystified by the combination, including, apparently, Iñaki himself; he showed up in Copenhagen possibly drunk and with no obvious recollection of what he had ordered. When he saw Pascal Barbot throwing away eel scraps, he took them and started making stock. 'It was like a David Copperfield illusion – no one thought that combination would work,' recalls Dave Chang. 'He fucking pulled that dish out of his ass.'

As service started, a sense of momentousness began to build. The chefs took turns plating each other's dishes, passing each other on the line with tentative grace. It was moving to watch: each of these great chefs, so long at the head of his own kitchen, sublimating himself to take on the task of the lowliest commis. And it was moving for them as well, the intense collaboration in the service of creativity. 'There was a moment around the third course,' says Daniel Patterson, 'when we were all like, "Holy shit, something's going on here."' That feeling grew as they approached the end, and Albert Adrià's dessert. 'This was the first time Albert had put on a chef's jacket since leaving elBulli,' Patterson says. 'I remember there was this amazing gold light coming through the windows, and we were all standing around him – the greatest pastry chef in the world – in complete silence, just staring.'

I could tell you about the food that night. About how the meal started with the small army of Noma's staff marching into the dining room, distributing the broom-sized bullrushes René had yanked from brackish water the day before. About the frisson that rippled through the dining room when the same servers put down Styrofoam ice cream containers on the tables and removed the covers to reveal heaps of tiny, still-live shrimp, their antennae waving madly ('I had wanted to serve them for the longest time, but it wasn't until Cook It Raw that I got up the courage to do it,' says Redzepi. 'What's more raw than live?') About the beautiful miniature landscape of earth, sea, and those previously-unknown herbs that constituted Patterson's dish. About the growing buzz in the room as Bottura's Pollution, as inkily ugly on the plate as it was delicious in the mouth, gave way to Bosi's sweet king crab dotted with wild herbs. About how everyone ran a lascivious tongue up the length of split cinnamon stick that contained Davide Scabin's rich veal tartare. About the elderflower honey that dripped languidly from Adria's microwaved sponge cake. But then I would be guilty of the same thing that I began this essay complaining about. And that night in Copenhagen was about much more than putting A into B.

When the meal was over, the chefs came out of the kitchen and danced a spontaneous conga line around a dining room convulsed in thunderous applause. It would be too obvious to call it release, but there was a kind of intense joy in that room that I had never before witnessed in a restaurant. It was the joy of transcendence, of connection, of finding your tribe. It was the joy of remembering why food and cooking and eating – all of them so necessary yet, in our world, so ridiculously fetishized – really matter. And above all else, it was the joy of being part of a moment that, even then, we knew would live in the memory of every single person lucky enough to be there that night.

Three years after that dinner, I sat with Albert in his new cocktail bar in Barcelona. By then, subsequent editions of Cook It Raw had been held in the far more exotic locales of Collio, Lapland, and Ishikawa, and Adrià had participated in all of them. But when I told him I was writing about the inaugural Cook It Raw, the one where we all went to Copenhagen with no idea of what lay ahead, he lit up like, well, like a middle-aged man recalling his first time. 'Ah,' he said wistfully. 'That's the one I'll never forget.'

Who'd have thought something so raw could produce so much heat?

A bus will take the chefs to Lammefjorden and Dragsholm Slot in the west of Zealand, where we will go foraging. The area is famous for the quality of its soil and the vast array of fresh vegetables and herbs grown there.

A

B 'We've picked lots of berries and lichen. Everyone's picked the same stuff, now everyone is trying to figure out what everyone else is doing so they can do a twist on it. But none of us are Scandinavian survival guides like René. He has an unfair advantage. Wait until we do this in New York.'

David Chang

A   Chefs and journalists gather in the gardens of Dragsholm Slot prior to the foraging expedition.

B   Spring onions (scallions) are plucked from the soil.

C   Claude and David kneel to investigate the local flora.

D   René leads the group to the foraging grounds.

E   Iñaki is introduced to the native plant life by Dragholms's chef, Claus Henriksen.

F   Sorrel, lovage and nettles are among the plants available to the chefs.

F

E

The chefs will arrive at Noma to begin preparation of their dishes for the evening's dinner. At midday a simple lunch will be served beside the canal. Journalists have a free morning.  The meal will commence at 19.00.

'Imagine boy scouts going to camp. Learning to tie new knots and see new places in the world and then seeing how we can bring back what we learnt and use it in our own kitchens – that's Cook It Raw.'

René Redzepi

A

A  The chefs enjoy an informal
    canal-side lunch before they start
    to prep the meal.

B  Claude examines the produce that
    he foraged on the previous day.

C

C　The staff at Noma work hard to
　prepare the front of house for the
　final meal.

D

E

F

D Massimo, Pascal and Davide discuss their dishes.

E Claude, Massimo and David enjoy the atmosphere of the kitchen.

F The curious residents of Noma's adjoining canal investigate the proceedings

G

H

G  René and his team prepare the bulrushes that he foraged the previous day.

H  David starts to prepare his dish.

I

J

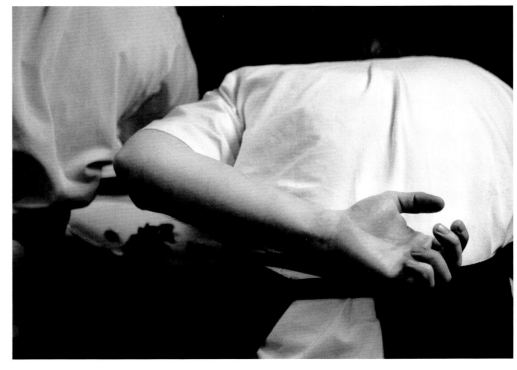

I   The chefs work together to plate up Daniel Patterson's dish.

J   The banter in the kitchen dies down and focus settles in as service nears.

K

L

M

N

K René watches in anticipation as the chefs take over his restaurant.

L Daniel scrutinizes the plates as his dish is pepared for service.

M Iñaki watches the activity in the kitchen whilst cooking at the stove.

N Albert relies on a steady hand to prepare his delicate dish.

'Cook It Raw is a message of hope in one way and in another way thinking deeply about where we are and what we are cooking. Tonight is an expression of the forest, the fish, the sea — what we did was try to preserve the quality of what we were serving and this is exactly the message.'

Massimo Bottura

O

P

O   René reflects on the meal after service is complete.

P   The chefs celebrate the success of the meal.

René Redzepi
Raw vegetables

René Redzepi
Salad of green strawberries and tree shoots

Ichiro Kubota
Shrimps with Kinome pepper and mousse of broad (fava) beans.
Limfjord oyster with Japanese citrus dressing. Turbot with five spices and venison sauce with Yuzu pepper

Daniel Patterson
Earth and sea

Massimo Bottura
Pollution – 20:30 Modena

Claude Bosi
King crab, pickled cucumber, white miso and wild flowers

David Chang
Hawthorne valley buttermilk and apple dashi with Dragsholm herbs

Pascal Barbot
Marinated mackerel, smoked eel and wild angelica

Iñaki Aizpitarte
Lobster, pigeon liver, chicken liver and wood sorrel

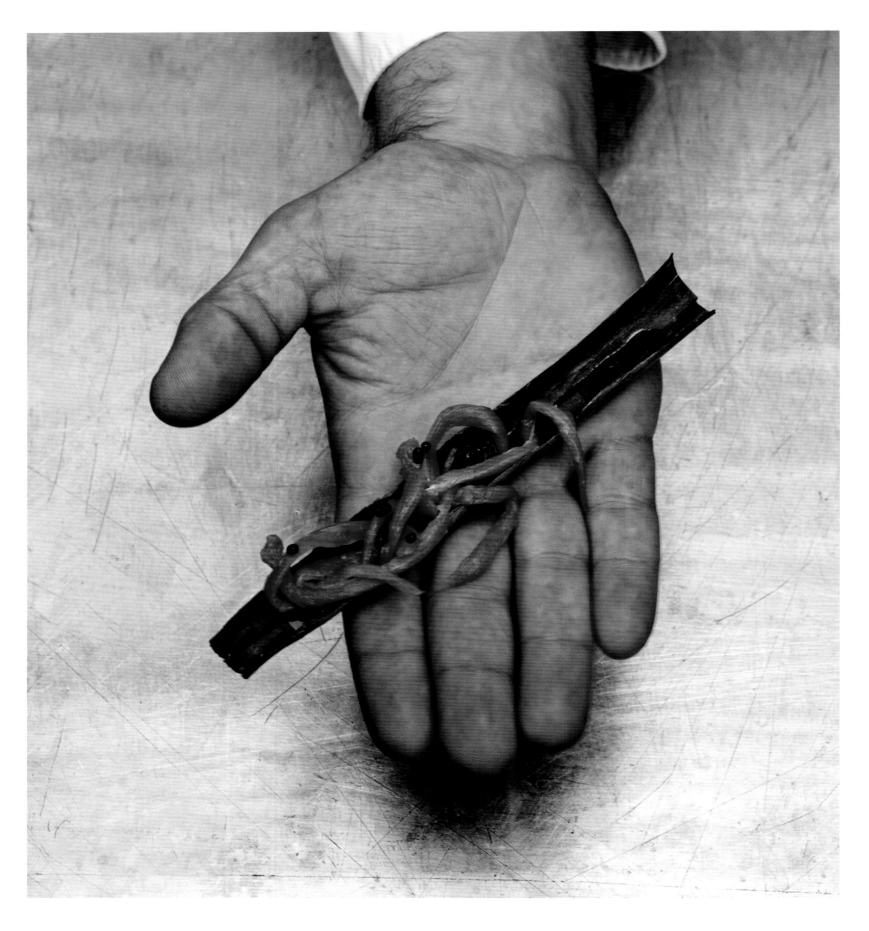

Davide Scabin
Steak Tartare B.C.

Joachim Wissler
Venison and jellyfied pumpernickel soup

Albert Adrià
40-second biscuit

P.45/46 – René Redzepi: Raw vegetables. Salad of green strawberries and tree shoots.

As the host, Redzepi was first out and produced four spectacular dishes. Spring radishes, carrots and green asparagus were presented on malt 'soil' with herb emulsion. A salad of green strawberries, spruce shoots and tender leaves of whitebeam and beech was served with fresh cream and black oil of burnt cucumber.

P.47 – Ichiro Kubota: Shrimps with Kinome pepper and mousse of broad (fava) beans. Limfjord oyster with Japanese citrus dressing. Turbot with five spices and venison sauce with Yuzu pepper.

At the first Cook It Raw event, Kubota used his undisputed expertise in raw seafood to prepare a dish full of variety, colour and taste, presenting three separate elements on one plate: a Limfjord oyster served in its half shell, a shot glass with shrimps in a green mousse, and a Japanese ceramic spoonful of spiced raw turbot. The focus was on the oyster, topped with a well-balanced combination of citric ponzu dressing, grated daikon, sweet soy and chives. Contrast to oyster was supplied by the creamy, sweet shrimp shot and the fresh, slightly spicy turbot.

P.48 – Daniel Patterson: Earth and sea: new harvest potatoes and coastal greens.

Daniel Patterson found inspiration for his dish in the similarities between his native coastal California and the Danish shores. It consisted of tiny potatoes, placed like pebbles on a beach of black volcanic sand – a ragout of squid ink and cucumber. Between the tender potatoes nestled small sprigs of fleshy samphire, adding crunchy texture and saltiness to them. The dish was finished with a few drops of Danish cold-pressed canola oil with a mild, nutty aroma of fresh peas.

P.49 – Massimo Bottura: Pollution – 20:30 Modena

Cuttlefish, raw cockles, monkfish liver and a puree of sea urchin roe, served in a dark green broth of samphire and other wild Danish herbs, topped by a foam of Sorrento lemons. The idea behind Bottura's dish was a gruesome environmental prediction: if marine pollution continues at the current rate, by 2050 the oceans will consist mainly of seaweed and giant squid. Why '20:30 Modena'? Bottura conceived the idea walking through his home town. His watch showed 20:30.

P.50 – Claude Bosi: King crab, pickled cucumber, white miso and wild flowers

Bosi's dish caught the essence of the raw theme in appearance, technique and taste. His main ingredient was the giant king crab, caught from the depths of the Norwegian Sea. He combined the cool, raw meat of the crab legs with earthy, sweet white miso paste and tiny Danish beach herbs and flowers. Cubes of pickled cucumber added acidity and texture to the pink crabmeat. Bosi considered the crab too delicate to cook and made the right choice. The dish was a true display of a perfect ingredient in its simple perfection.

P.51 – David Chang: Hawthorne valley buttermilk and apple dashi with Dragsholm herbs

For this, probably the most subtle dish of the event, Chang made his own interpretation of dotorimuk – Korean acorn jelly. He got the idea by imagining that his Korean ancestors had arrived in Denmark two hundred years earlier. He switched the acorns by substituting milk and made a dairy version of the classic Korean dish. The soft, silken jelly was surrounded by a dense reduction of apple and konbu kelp with toasted pine nuts. It was finished with wild herbs from the surroundings of Dragsholm Castle: wood sorrel, common sorrel, and tiny, white ramsons flowers to add small bursts of garlicky aroma.

P.52 – Pascal Barbot: Marinated mackerel, smoked eel and wild angelica

Marinated mackerel with raw turnip and a soup of wild angelica with smoked eel. The fresh mackerel was firmed up in a marinade and served with a mild but aromatic confit of lemon. Barbot added a wedge of turnip covered in sesame seeds for fresh crunch, texture and sweetness to the lemony and salty fish, which was decorated with an array of wild green herbs and flowers. A tiny cup of moss green herb soup with smoked eel was served apart as a contrast to the main dish.

P.53 – Iñaki Aizpitarte: Lobster, pigeon liver, chicken liver and wood sorrel

Lightly poached lobster with a clear stock of smoked mackerel and rice vinegar served with a paste of raw pigeon and chicken livers topped with grated orange zest, pistachios and fresh wood sorrel. Aizpitarte picked the prized Danish black lobster as his main ingredient. True to his bold cooking style, he paired the lobster meat with a slightly bitter paste of pigeon and chicken livers. He added tang to the dish with grated orange zest and finished it with some smoky stock and one of the foraged signature herbs of the New Nordic Kitchen, the citrusy, acidic wood sorrel.

P.54 – Davide Scabin: Steak tartare B.C.

Filaments of veal with black caviar served in cinnamon bark. Visually, Scabin's dish was undoubtedly the most stunning dish of the first Cook It Raw event. His chefs had cut the veal shoulder into 1,800 individual filaments, a laborious process that took sixty hours. Scabin presented the dish as a personal and provocative statement about the use of time instead of energy. 'Who is richer,' asked Scabin 'The busy man with the money to hire people to cut his meat, or the poor man who has no money but has time to do the job?'

P.55 – Joachim Wissler: Venison and jellyfied pumpernickel soup

Most of the chefs chose their ingredients from the Nordic seas and the Danish coastline, so German chef Joachim Wissler of Vendôme decided to do something different and went for the gamey, mature taste of raw venison. He combined it with several of his favourite ingredients: almonds, hazelnuts, tiny chanterelles, morels and cherries, which added mature woodland flavours to the dish. The influences of German cuisine were clear, emphasized by a soup of malty pumpernickel bread served in the form of a spicy liquid jelly. The blood-red venison was wrapped in a thin sheet of cured speck, bringing the taste of fat to the lean meat.

P.56 – Albert Adrià: 40-second biscuit

A sponge cake served with pine nut oil, elderflower sorbet, acacia honey and fresh elder flowers. Adrià's idea was to catch the aromas of the Danish summer in a fresh, floral sorbet. For the sponge cake he deviated slightly from the event's theme of limited energy use by cooking it, but compromised by using a microwave, the quickest and most efficient of cooking methods, for a mere forty seconds. And then, to make amends, Adrià claimed to have churned the sorbet by hand.

## Cook It Raw and Nature – by René Redzepi

By organising the first Cook It Raw to coincide with the 2009 United Nations Climate Change Conference, Andrea Petrini, Alessandro Porcelli and myself were, in retrospect, making a statement. The conference, which was held in my home city of Copenhagen, sought to bring together the nations of the world and address the important issue of how to reduce greenhouse gas emissions for future generations. Many of the journalists who joined us in Copenhagen, fuelled by the conference's

agenda, latched on to Cook It Raw's 'no energy' theme and reported the resulting dishes as politically charged edible responses to climate change. However, that initial edition of Raw was far more about creating an opportunity for cooks to see new things – an unknown terroir laden with unfamiliar ingredients – than it was a political reaction to the conference. As a group of like-minded people who all believe that good cooking starts with great ingredients, I was also hoping a visit to Denmark would help some of my fellow chefs realise that great products are everywhere, even somewhere like here, which is not traditionally recognised for its culinary heritage.

The idea was to promote the idea that every landscape, no matter how seemingly barren or remote, is home to a larder of ingredients that can fuel the stomachs and creativity of any chef. In the past, the experience of eating at a fine-dining restaurant was inevitably punctuated by the appearance of a handful of luxury items, many of which had often travelled thousands of miles before landing on the diner's plate;

truffles, fois gras, caviar. The heightened sense of eco consciousness and increasing awareness in sustainability that has been prevalent in recent years has changed this and the cult of the locavore is spreading. More and more, chefs are looking to their own environments to source ingredients and inspiration for their cooking, a change that is not the result of a fad or trend, but that is born out of necessity.

This approach to cooking means that every component of a dish is treated with respect and no one ingredient is more important than the others. Because the concept of terroir means that a landscape is defined by what grows there, the humble vegetable has been elevated from supporting act to centre stage. Seasonality and locality are central to controlling and maintaining the quality of ingredients, which means that the food that locavore chefs are able to produce is very much dictated by their location and the time of year. By ensuring that we only cook with local produce that can be plucked from the earth and in our kitchens within a number of hours, we can transform these seemingly simple ingredients into truly remarkable dishes.

One of the most interesting things about this approach to cooking is that it forces the chef to reengage with their immediate environment and the food of their homeland. It's not about placing limitations on chefs, but simply asking them to take stock of what is available around them, rather than immediately looking elsewhere. There are many ingredients the world over that have fallen out of fashion or are still waiting to be discovered, which makes this style of cooking very exciting. With this in mind, it is important to make the distinction that we do not cook Danish cuisine at Noma; we cook Danish ingredients. Some of the produce that we use would never be found in a Danish supermarket, had never been used in cooking at all until we decided to experiment with them.

Around the time of the first Cook It Raw, it seemed as if gastronomic innovation revolved around the newest machinery or latest technological marvel. Like many restaurants, I couldn't afford such equipment and, back then, I didn't have the resources to investigate how to use them. Such limitations led me to consider how I could cook food that feels forward thinking and has its own identity. At the same time, there was a movement towards regimentation in the kitchen – against impulse. Menus were preciously planned out well in advance, dishes added into rotation only when each and every gram of salt had been weighed

out. A new class of more perfunctory cooks was being raised. It was as if even the chefs themselves were becoming more mechanical. But great cooking can never be robotic – it requires soul, intuition and originality. Whilst the current styles of cooking undoubtedly required great technical skill, they did not excite me. So I started to look for a style of cooking that suited my bountiful aspirations and limited resources.

The most practical and natural solution was to follow my intuition, taking a far more organic approach and using what was around me, taking advantage of where I was – being reactive to the seasons and my surroundings. I hoped that this would enable us to realise new 'letters' and expand our seemingly limited culinary alphabet.

My own experience of trying to populate Noma's kitchen with native Danish ingredients was marked by moments of epiphany, with each new discovery driving our enthusiasm, and the food we were able to produce, to greater heights. At that time, even we believed that the plant kingdom had left us Danes with little more than the uninspiring roots, onions and cabbages that were, at that time, synonymous with our cuisine. Using spices was out of the question; they were exotic, foreign condiments from distant lands and the harsh Nordic winter left the ground devoid of produce for several months of the year. Then there came a moment of revelation; we found some sea arrowgrass growing on a beach one cold, windy morning. The secretive herb was hidden, nestled amidst a clump of hostile beach grasses, but its flavour was so profound and delicious that it was more than worth the effort of finding it. I remember racing back to the restaurant, as excited as a child and desperate for all the boys in the kitchen to taste it too. They couldn't believe it. Could it really be possible that we could taste coriander? The flavour that we knew so well from Thai and from Latin American cuisine, masquerading as a harsh little shrub and hiding out on the shoreline of our very own city. The discovery, at that time, fueled us in so many ways. I remember asking myself if coriander is right there, what other flavours remain to be unearthed around us? There were other experiences similar to this of course and the sum of all of them has made much of our success possible. They have continuously rekindled our inspiration and given us renewed momentum. To me, interacting with nature – using your instincts and sensibilities, being constantly curious, exploring the unexplored – is a way of moving forward. It is one of the ways that Noma moves forward.

Respecting the land also means respecting those that work on it and look after it. One of the earliest and most important relationships that I formed with my suppliers was with the farmer Søren Wiuff. He cultivated carrots and other odd vegetables for himself and a few small restaurants. Seeing and tasting those peculiar and special ingredients, putting my own hands in the earth that they grew in, captivated my imagination, fired my curiosity

and influenced how I cook today. Søren is now one of the restaurant's principal suppliers and I owe a great debt to the produce that he grows and the dedication, passion and inquisitive enthusiasm that he puts into it.

In inviting eleven chefs to Copenhagen for the first Cook It Raw, in asking them to leave what they knew at home and to work with unusual products and rely only on their intuition and skills as cooks, I was hoping they would be inspired – just as my early experiences with Wiuff inspired me. With this in mind, we – this motley, rag-tag crew – clambered through the woods and meadows around Dragsholm Castle outside Copenhagen. I still recall, very vividly, when David Chang came to a halt as he crept through the forest, the expression on his face changing as the once simple scenery around him became a generous larder. I remember, too, the moment that Davide Scabin fell in love with wild garlic – calling it 'sexy' as he shook his hips suggestively – and how Albert Adrià giggled like a big kid every time he came across a new aromatic herb or delicious flower. Taking these chefs out of the comfort of their own kitchens and introducing them to the deliciousness of wild places was personally very satisfying. One of the greatest rewards of foraging for yourself – which I was happy to see people realise here – is that you are able to look at the world differently. We may not have strictly set out to make nature the event's main attraction, but it was clear that it had to be part of Cook It Raw's agenda going forward.

There are other motivations behind Cook It Raw that have a less tangible value to the world at large but are ultimately the reason that we keep going back. At these events we are surrounded by like-minded friends, safe from judging eyes, we were allowed to make mistakes without worry, to screw up and laugh at ourselves. In our real lives, failure isn't an option. Running a restaurant that's full everyday with hundreds of people waiting for a table, being responsible for the duties, progress and wellbeing of the many under you, you yourself constantly under the scrutiny of journalists, guide books, voters, co-workers, we are not allowed any margin for error. People can wait months for a table at a restaurant and it is the chef's job to give them an experience that is worth the wait, that is worthy of their expectations and hard-earned money. Cook It Raw offers a brief respite from this stress and responsibility – a short retreat from reality. We are free to play, free to fail and thus free to learn. This openness and humility have brought us closer together too. We have become firm friends and this has undoubtedly contributed to making sure that Cook It Raw is not just another one-off event.

A chef's life is framed by kitchen services, days structured by recipes and measured through painful corporeal assessment – cuts, burns and other customary accidents are all that detach us from our grueling routine. Knives, pots and pans offer no comfort, no sympathy. It is at Cook It Raw that we have found some tenderness and camaraderie, a little warmth. These friendships are about more than comradeship and a sense of belonging though, they also drive our food forward. Many of us are like-minded in our approach to cooking and sourcing ingredients, and by sharing our discoveries and experiences we are also able to keep our enthusiasm alive. By sharing our dreams and stories of discovery we can start to gain a picture of just how many untapped sustainable resources the natural world has to offer – Alex Atala scours the Amazon for new ingredients that will bring the soul of Brazil to his plates and Magnus Nilsson spends his summers preserving the produce he harvests around Fäviken so that he can use local ingredients during Sweden's harsh winter months. Each of us shares a vision that is skewed only by the environments in which we cook and the unique produce that are on offer in them. We are not trying to put the brakes on culinary progress, just divert the tracks slightly. Making the best of the ingredients of our native lands, those that are the easiest to access and are of the best quality, and finding new ways of using them in our food.

Through subsequent editions of Cook It Raw – from Copenhagen to Italy, Lapland and Japan – discovering the local landscape and discerning the edible have indeed provided a common thread.

In Copenhagen I showed off the delights of my country's larder by leading a forage, introducing the group to the many wild ingredients that grow along the Danish coastline. At that first event, I served up freshly picked bulrushes and live fjordshrimp, challenging the diners to reevaluate their conception of what is edible.

In Collio, the producers of the region once again took centre stage. We met local farmers and sampled the rare Rosa di Gorizia, a beautiful radicchio that grows only in this remote region of northern Italy – seemingly delicate, but capable of growing in the dead of winter. We also visited local winemakers who stunned us with their delicious vintages made from local grapes.

In Lapland we fished, foraged and hunted in the harsh Finnish landscape. We watched a reindeer slaughtered and saw how every part of the beast, from its hide to its milk, went on to sustain the area's native people – it was traumatic and humbling and taught us the true value of life and food.

Japan provided the greatest sense of displacement for most of the group and here we were introduced to a culture who truly understand the importance of using the best quality ingredients and treating them with absolute care. We plucked wild wasabi straight from the riverbed, saw sushi masters at work and were instructed in the best techniques for slaughtering fish.

Each experience was totally special, totally unique and totally of that place. That's the way food should be.

Clearly, on a personal level the power of the Cook It Raw collective is felt very keenly. We each return to our kitchens refreshed, inspired and with renewed perspective. But we do return to our kitchens. We're chefs at the end of the day, not activists. So, what can Cook It Raw really say and do to give nature the attention it deserves?

Cook it Raw's chefs all agree that nature is the mother of cooking. We know that you can't create great flavours out of bad ingredients and that the best ingredients can only be found in the healthiest of ecologies. Each environment that we have visited during a Cook It Raw event has been totally unique, from the ingredients that are on offer to the culture of its people. Nature is what defines both of these things - the environment, the climate, the landscape all combine to give each place its challenging uniqueness. These places are remote and untouched. These places are Raw.

By continuing to introduce chefs to unique, vibrant environments around the world and the incredible ingredients found there I hope we'll inspire them to return home and explore the biodiversity on their own doorsteps. This doesn't just apply to the chefs invited to the event, but also to those who read about it, those who are inspired by it. The next generation of chefs are growing up in an era when issues such as seasonality and sustainability are at the forefront of the social consciousness, and not just in terms of food.

So, Cook It Raw is about spreading a message, raising awareness and inspiring the next generation of cooks. Some of their discoveries might land up on their menu for you to try and in trying these unfamiliar ingredients I hope it will encourage you to consider that if we want delicious food in the future we all have to start caring about where this food comes from. We need to look after nature and our environment if we expect it to keep looking after us.

# Cook It Raw (II)

## THE DINNERS:

**[I]**          Denmark
         N A T U R E
    Zero energy cooking

Cook It Raw's inaugural dinner in Copenhagen sees the chefs explore nature through a zero energy cooking challenge.

**[II]**          Italy
      C R E A T I V I T Y
    Chef versus winter

During the depths of a Collio winter Cook It Raw's chefs prepare dinner in an experiment of creativity.

**[III]**         Finland
    C O L L A B O R A T I O N
    Cooking in the wild

Cook It Raw heads into the Lappish wilds to test the strength of the brotherhood by holding a collaborative dinner.

**[IV]**          Japan
      F U T U R E
   Avant-garde meets tradition

The chefs meet the producers and crafts men of Ishikawa to create a Cook It Raw dinner that marries avant-garde cooking with tradition.

## THE PRINCIPLES:

[I]   Nature rules
[II]   Limitations boost creativity

[III]   Collaboration not competition
[IV]   Look back to look forward

## THE CHEFS:

| | | |
|---|---|---|
| ✘ | Albert Adrià | ES |
| ✘ | Iñaki Aizpitarte | FR |
| ✘ | Alex Atala | BR |
| ○ | Fredrik Andersson | SE |
| ✘ | Pascal Barbot | FR |
| ○ | Mark Best | AU |
| ✘ | Claude Bosi | UK |
| ✘ | Massimo Bottura | IT |
| ○ | Sean Brock | US |
| ✘ | David Chang | US |
| ○ | Mauro Colagreco | AR |
| ✘ | Quique Dacosta | ES |
| ○ | Alexandre Gauthier | FR |

| | | |
|---|---|---|
| ○ | Ichiro Kubota | JP |
| ✘ | Yoshihiro Narisawa | JP |
| ○ | Magnus Nilsson | SE |
| ✘ | Petter Nilsson | SE |
| ✘ | Daniel Patterson | US |
| ✘ | René Redzepi | DK |
| ✘ | Davide Scabin | IT |
| ○ | Ben Shewry | XX |
| ○ | Kondo Takahiko | JP |
| ○ | Yoji Tokuyoshi | JP |
| ○ | Hans Välimäki | FI |
| ○ | Joachim Wissler | DE |

Cook It Raw reconvenes in Collio Goriziano, in Friuli-Venezia Giulia Italy during the depths of winter. With temperatures a cruel -5°C and little in the way of fresh produce the chefs are challenged to prepare an elaborate dinner in an experiment of creativity.

Austria

Milan

Turin

Slovenia

A

C

B

Collio

Rome

Naples

Area:
7,858 km²

Population, Persons:
1,235,270

Population Density:
Persons per km²
160

Power Consumed:
kWh per household
7,750

(A)
Pri Lojzetu
restaurant
(near AjdovšĐinam,
Slovenia):
Where the chefs
held their opening-
night meal

(B)
Border with
Slovenia:
Where the chefs
went wild boar
hunting

(C)
Gorizia:
Where the chefs
visited the local
food market and
met local producers

## Raw Ingredients

With the ground too hard and bare for foraging the chefs visit Collio's farmers' market to pick up produce for the closing night's dinner:

**Meat:**
Beef
Boar
Rabbit
Hare
Chicken
Game birds
Pork
Venison

**Fish:**
Eel
Cockles
Sea bass
Sole
Turbot

**Dairy:**
Ewe's milk,
ricotta and cheeses
Cow's milk,
ricotta and cheeses
Goat's milk,
ricotta and cheeses

**Herbs:**
Burdock
Curly leaf
mustard
Wild mint
Evening primrose
Garden sorrel
Broad leaf dock
Salsify

Sage
Rosemary
Thyme
Marjoram

**Vegetables/Salad:**
Cabbages
Raddichio
Turnip
Jerusalem Artichoke

**Fruit:**
Apples
Pears
Persimmon

## Wine Production in Collio
## (Thousands of Hectoliters)

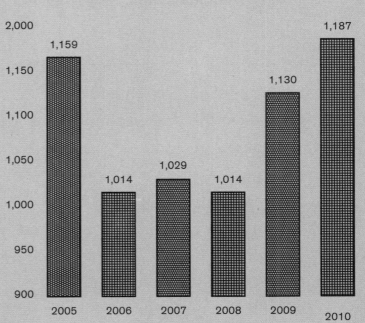

## Climate Graph
## (Left: Max/Min C°, Right: Days)

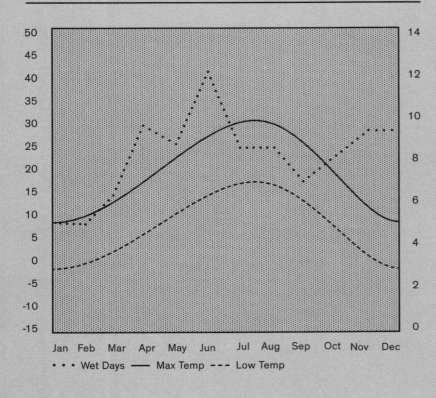

• • • Wet Days    —— Max Temp    --- Low Temp

## Radicchio

There are many varieties, here are the ones considered most important:

Radicchio Rosso di Treviso:
(Comes in two varieties: Precoce and Tardivo)
Radicchio Variegato di Castelfranco
Radicchio Rosso di Chioggia
Radicchio Rosso di Verona

When winter is hard it takes a special kind of producer to make anything grow. Cook It Raw's chefs take their inspiration from the resourcefulness of local producers. Lucio Brumat, who grows the rare 'Gorizia Rose' radicchio and Josko Gravner who produces stand out wines from Ribolla Gialla and Breg grapes.

The wet mist on the laguna carried a dark allure that morning in the shape of the local cinghiale (wild boars) that lurked just a few foggy mountaintops away. The call of these beasts had proven too difficult to resist for Alex Atala, the Brazilian hunter.

Cooking and eating in the wilderness of the barren and brutal Italian/Slovenian border is not exactly a walk in the park, it's more of a walk on the hillside.

But hunting there, that's a walk on the wild side. Not that the cinghiale see it as the wild side, they are as evasive in Collio as anywhere else on the planet. The boar can have a ferocious temperament – charging head first at you, pissed off because you woke them up and pissed off because the winter is so fucking hard food-wise. But, in Collio, it is the creatures guarding the boar that you really have to look out for. These guards are Slovenian woodsmen and they too are pissed off because winter is so fucking hard food-wise. In this instance, they were also pissed off at the arrival of a bright-eyed and enthusiastic Brazilian chef, who obviously thought he could eat food from the same plate as them. The actual plate here being a dividing mountain between rich Italy and not so rich Slovenia, and the food in question being covered in fur and resembling a prehistoric pig.

The news that Alex the Hunter had been kidnapped by some Slovenian locals reached a few of us whilst we were visiting a small island on a nearby Laguna. The steaming spoonfuls of delicious fish soup that were about to enter our mouths froze midair as the story unraveled via the medium of a mobile phone. Arms were waved, heads were twisted, nails were bitten. We feared the worst. Perhaps fuelled by the spirit of Pier Paolo Pasolini, the controversial film director, intellectual and former owner of the hut we were eating our soup in, some of us had already twisted the details into a sodomising drama. Luckily, and with only his pride bruised, Alex was soon returned to us. It made for a good story while we enjoyed those soup though.

The reason we had travelled to the Laguna was not only to slurp soup and speculate about the fate of a dear friend. We had primarily gone to fish. The evening's dinner was looming and we were responsible for supplying the raw materials. If we failed to catch enough fish we would go hungry.

Our boats slowly snaked their way up the stream in search of food. We felt a bit like the eels in the legendary dish 'An eel swimming up the river Po' created by the Italian modernist master of cuisine Massimo Bottura (who sported an oversized Borsalino for the trip and won a prize for most stylish fishing hat that stands unthreatened since that day). We were escorted by the Carabinieri (Italian military police), which offered no small reassurance after Alex's adventures with the locals. Despite the ominous presence of the police and the imposing shadow cast by Massimo's hat we did not scare off the fish and our haul was plentiful.

Piggy in the middle.
Watching a pig get killed and slaughtered is a harrowing experience. After all, pigs are our friends and almost like family. Cannibals have testified that humans taste like pigs. And that's not metaphorically speaking. We gathered together outside an abattoir and two men carefully tried to wrestle a pig into submission, but the pig knew our game. First try, no success. The pig screamed wildly with a sound that cuts through time and memory. Second try, bang. Our friend had begun his journey towards our plates and stomachs. Swiftly the two men started cutting up the steaming pig, its inner heat steaming as it met Collio's frigid fog. Seeing the reaction of this group of hardened chefs and food journalists was a revelation. We were all, myself included, shocked and saddened by the short but brutal few minutes of piggy screaming. This made us all reflect on why we eat and why death is so off-putting to someone who cooks and eats for a living. If you can't handle the death of a friend, don't eat him.

Recovery came quickly and we all joined together over the grill. The freshly butchered pork from every corner of this animal was cooked to perfection. Nothing was wasted. Eating and cooking in this way may appear primitive, but is probably much more sophisticated from an ethical and gastronomical perspective than most other food that was being served in restaurants all over the world at that moment. Charles Darwin would have approved, probably Friedrich Nietsche too, and certainly Pier Paolo Pasolini.

Backbone man.
He walked towards us with a big welcoming smile, clad in a wool cape, and a felt hat. He looked like he had just come off set from acting in an imaginary film about glorious mountainous partisan resistance towards aggressive intruders. Josko Sirk is a natural ambassador of the hillside – a real Don. His handshake was firm, his hug was warm, his eyes were sparkling with genuine curiosity and good will. He and his family run a restaurant called La Subida just a mile from the Slovenian border on the Italian side.

Everyone you meet in Collio gets a sparkle in their eyes and an expansive smile when you mention the name of Josko or his restaurant. The restaurant itself blends seamlessly with the landscape; fashioned from natural wood and stone, the outside walls lined up with the trees that populate the immediate landscape. The minimalist glass veranda was delicately lit and made the perfect place for a drink and some snacks before the long and hearty dinner that awaited us.

Eating in La Subida is like eating at the table of your grandparents. If only they could cook this well, that is. A welcoming fireplace is the centre of attention in the dining room, not only for warmth and quiet entertainment, but also for cooking the renowned polenta which graces a lot of the dishes. Josko Sirk has invented a hypnotic mechanical device for stirring the cornflour in a pot over the fire, the mesmerizing rhythm gradually exciting your appetite. Should you ever visit La Subida, and I sincerely recommend that you do, then please look out for the stinco di vitello (slow cooked veal shank). It has a subtle smokiness, a slight caramelization, and is a masterclass in showing off all the succulence and variation in texture that a veal shank can possibly have. La Subida has one of the most extensive local wine lists in the region and, if you allow the sommelier to choose for you, the possibilities of finding something rare and seemingly undiscovered are nearly endless. Should you get the chance to try game birds whilst in season, then do ask for them in La Subida; Josko Sirk is not only a chef but also a keen and responsible hunter.

Despite the delicious food and excellent wine, Josko Sirk is most renowned for his vinegar. He makes this elegant and versatile natural product himself, not too far away from the restaurant. His production line is certainly not a factory, more of tiny winery with open air vats where the home-made natural wine slowly evolves, with absolutely nothing added, into a juicy amber-colour vinegar. This was one of the best vinegars I have ever tasted, it holds power and silky astringency in just a few drops. Sirk is one of those rare artisans who looks beyond his own borders and sees friends where others see enemies. The appreciation and respect for Josko Sirk and his family permeates Collio's hills and woodlands, and it probably will continue to do so for generations to come.

A rose, but not a rose.
A truly unique product from the Collio region is the Rosa di Gorizia, which got its name from the nearby town. The tender leaves of this rare and delicious radicchio sprout gently towards the sun in deepest winter. The field where they are cultivated is in perfect order, ensuring the protection and support of this delicate little flower-shaped morsel. The elegant radicchio looks out of place surrounded by stones and gravel and their earthy tones of beige, ochre and dark brown. But there it was, bright purple and darkish red, the size of a grown up's hand. Striking in colour, offset by the barren land, I imagine that the Rosa di Gorizia can be detected from space (or at least a low flying plane). Its taste is slightly bitter, like a normal radicchio, but slightly softer. The texture is slightly crunchy and a sweetness is revealed in its aftertaste. Still, a radicchio it is. But a proud radicchio, a delicious sole survivor, an exclusive standalone artifact in the world of winter

vegetables. Give it some space and time, and you will remember it forever.

Wine should be orange.
Collio (and for that matter, the neighbouring mountain of Carso) is a particularly deep but thin little pocket in the world of wine. Before my visit for Cook It Raw, I had barely heard of these wines (to a non-Italian Collio is just a fraction of Friuli) but the multi-facetted colours of Collio's own distinct identity shone brightly once I was there. Meeting the legendary Josko Gravner was nothing short of a revelation. He is a slow wine maker, in the best possible sense: constantly rethinking his sharp and philosophical application to wine making, going back and forth in time and history. He has solely rediscovered the ancient Georgian technique of making wine in amfora vases. These enormous and fairly porous vessels are dug into the ground of his pared down cellar, filled with juice from his beloved grape Ribolla Gialla. A thin layer of beeswax lines the inside of the vases and helps the wine develop slowly but surely. These precious grapes are macerated not only for a few days or weeks but for seven months. On the surface this seems insanely risky and nobody before Josko had dared to mature their grapes for that long. It turns out that Josko was right, and he can now offer a wine that is like nothing else on the planet. Faint scents of mandarin, saffron, mature lemon, perhaps a hint of buttery cep, outstanding length and a mouthfeel that whispers that this wine is for keeping. Who could have guessed that ancient wine making would be the most modern? Well, you should ask all of the wine makers who are now being inspired by him all across Europe. Marco Perco, the quiet wine maker from the Roncus, who seemingly never stops improving his wines. A man with a strong social awareness, helpful in every way and aspect. A multi talent with a palette for wine making that should be recognized worldwide. Precise, sharp, generous, minerally driven from the core and nerve of Collio, both him and his wines are unforgettable. But it was another slow macerated orange wine from Radikon that was chosen for Cook It Raw. At the final dinner, Iñaki Aizpitarte poured it into his green soup, crowning it with croutons and lardo, and proclaiming in the kitchen afterwards 'I looove wine', as if we didn't know this already. Half of the bottle went into the soup, half of the bottle went into the chef.

Cool in Collio.
When I think of Collio, the first and last person that springs to my mind is the energetic Carla Capalbo. An American-Italian living in London and beyond, who has documented the life of living in Collio better and more thoroughly than any insider in modern times. Her inquisitive nature has brought her back to the vineyards and artisan producers of these hills and mountains again and again. Her love for the orange wines of Josko Gravner, Radikon and Damijan Podversic has enamored the outside

world via numerous articles and a prize-winning book. Without Carla's personal interest and devoted sharing of contacts, the trip wouldn't have happened.

The whole region of Collio carries a certain underlying borderline mystique. Why? Perhaps because the towering cultural ego of nearby Venice casts its shadow over these luscious hillsides in a somewhat condescending way. Perhaps it's because the collective mentality here is brushed with memories of war and division, perhaps because the land is stony and barren at parts, perhaps because the strong winds create strong characters. Perhaps the Collio region is a bit special, due to the open-minded attitude towards its past, which is has acted as a gate between westernized Italy and easternized Slovenia. If not a Siamese twin culture, one that is at least separated at birth. You can easily tell that you are travelling through an agricultural society here; the towns are small and the streets are narrow, full of macellerias, pasticcerias and wine bars. Meeting points, cultural joints and ligaments are testament to the necessity and joy of eating what the local land has to offer.

The wind blows hard in Collio, it creeps underneath your skin. It's not for everyone to visit and enjoy. It's for the adventurous outsider, the personality who has seen, say, Tuscany one time too many. The traveler who doesn't want beach resorts and conventional luxury, who has had enough with hoards of people camera permanently in hand. Collio is for the peaceful minded, for the person interested in hard to find human values, in artisan culture. The person interested in discovering unusual wine and amazing food from a slightly colder climate than most believe Italy is home to. Collio is for the traveler looking for a subtle and long-lasting fruity acidity, not for the tourist looking for artificial sweetness.

The chefs travel to Gorizia where they sample herbs with Giusi Foschia, a visionary grower/gatherer from the region. The group then visit Lucio Brumat, one of the last producers of the beautiful Gorizia Rose radicchio.

A

B

A  Iñaki Aizpitarte scours the ground for herbs to use in his soup.

B  René Redzepi dissects one of his finds.

C

C   The Gorizia rose is one of the rarest and most expensive salad vegetables in the world.

The chefs will be escorted to Grado Lagoon where they will spend the morning fishing for fish and eels. There will also be a boat trip around the stunning lagoon.

A

B   'Talking about raw is talking about the relationship we have with the product, the producer of that product, the farmer, the hunter, the fisherman.'

Massimo Bottura

A   Massimo Bottura gets up close and personal with his catch.

B   The Grado Lagoon is teaming with fish, such as these sea bass.

The chefs will witness a pig slaughter and butcher. The meat from the animal will be barbecued for lunch and the chefs will be invited to bid in an auction of its innards.

A

' It was totally disturbing. If you raised that pig or grew that vegetable and you saw someone treating it with disrespect (after it was killed) you'd be upset. I think its part of our job as cooks and chefs to reflect the energy, the effort that went in the producing it by making it as delicious as possible. To cook it with as much integrity as possible. To really appreciate food you have to know the full cycle of life.'

David Chang (after the pig slaughter)

A   The butcher proudly displays the pig's head after its slaughter.

The chefs will travel to the evening venue La Subida to commence
preparations for the final dinner. Free afternoon for all others.
The final meal will commence at 20:30.

A

B

'At the end of the first Cook It Raw we were all friends and we've remained friends. This is good because the food world is changing and it's important to have a community to share ideas.'

Daniel Patterson

C

A　Massimo Bottura explains the concept for his dish to the group.

B　Narisawa examines the dish that his course will be served on.

C　Daniel Patterson and Pascal Barbot consult before getting started.

D

F

E

D   René Redzepi starts to plate up.

E   Quique Dacosta prepares the seaweed for his dish.

F   René samples Iñaki Aizpitarte's soup.

G

H

'Cook It Raw is a way for the chefs to break away from their routines and environment, which has to be super controlled. These guys are playing the world soccer final every night, every lunch everything they do has to be perfect. Everything has to be perfect in an environment that isn't perfect. Raw materials aren't there, chefs are sick, customers are obnoxious – there are so many factors that they have to contend with. When they are at Cook It Raw they get to break away from all of this.'

Alessandro Porcelli

G H    Claude Bosi, David Chang and Petter Nilsson enjoy the convivial atmosphere in the kitchen.

I    The chestnuts for Narisawa's dish are toasted under a blow torch.

# Recette Pascal Barbot
## Cook it raw

*Intitulé de la recette : Artichaut épineux, truffe et pomelo, noix-parmesan*

- 55 artichaut épineux d'Italie (1 par personne = 55)
- acide ascorbique ou citrique
- 500 g de brisures de truffe noire (tuber melanospurum) fraiche
- quelque salade amère de la région (type radicchio)
- 20 citron jaune (extra top)
- 2 l huile olive fruitée vert Italie
- Fleur de sel
- Poivre du moulin
- 5 bottes de persil plat
- 500 g de Parmesan extra
- 500 g de beurre demi-sel
- Thym, ail, laurier, romarin,
- Herbes sauvage

Texte :

Même dans la rudesse de l'hiver ; les épines, l'amertume, le froid, l'isolement ; des moments de joie restent possibles !!! Une éclaircie, un cœur d'artichaut : donne un peu d'amour à chaque personne qui semble digne d'intérêt. *"Cœur d'artichaut, une feuille pour tout le monde"*.

Seul les épines résistent au grand froid sur les ronciers. Comme son nom l'indique « artichaut épineux » ses grosses épines sont très présentes sur la structure de ce légume, un centre végétal, le cœur. Sortie de l'hiver, noix, parmesan sont des produits de longue conservation, l'amertume de la truffe noire est contente de rencontrer un copain : le fruité « pomelo des îles Marquises » !!! Bonjour soleil !!!

K

L

J   Petter Nilsson and the other chefs help to plate up René's dish.

K   A pensive Iñaki enjoys a well-deserved glass of wine as the dinner comes to a close.

L   All of the diners attending the meal were asked to bring their own forks.

Massimo Bottura
We should never stop planting

Alex Atala
Baby squid with priprioca sauce

Quique Dacosta
Oyster with seaweed

Iñaki Aizpitarte
Raw peasant soup en chabrot

Petter Nilsson
Where the wild boars are

Yoshihiro Narisawa
Evolve with the forest

Daniel Patterson
Imagining Collio from California

Pascal Barbot
Moments of joy

David Chang
40 north, 120 west

Claude Bosi
Brass monkeys

René Redzepi
The Jensen`s hard winter of 1941

Albert Adrià
Apple rose with an ice cream heart

Davide Scabin
The dynamics of ox and hen

## P.84 — Massimo Bottura: We should never stop planting

Roe buck meat, seeds, nuts, sprouts, truffles and Jerusalem artichoke. Bottura's dish was the dinner's opener, and he made a profound statement while presenting it: 'If we don't keep the woods and countryside the way they are, we'll be doing irreparable damage to our future resources,' he declared. He had cured the meat of a young goat, cut it into strips and served it with a small landscape of sprouts, seeds, nuts and Jerusalem artichoke. There was a colourful and dramatic detail on the serving plate of white rock: blood fingerprints, made with beet juice.

## P.85 — Alex Atala: Baby squid with priprioca sauce

Brazilian chef Atala's dish at the dinner held in the wine cellar of Villa Russiz was a simple piece of art served on a slab of grey rock. Three baby squid from the Adriatic with beautifully speckled skin were served with a blood-red puree of beetroot spiced with the aromatic Amazonian priprioca root. Although the squid appeared to be raw, Atala had prepared them by what he called one of the 'forgotten techniques'. He had placed them in buckets of iced seawater and shaken the buckets vigorously, giving the squid a firm and slightly crunchy texture.

## P.86 — Quique Dacosta: Oyster with seaweed

Spanish chef Dacosta presented a dish reminiscent of a small mouthful of beautifully flavoured seawater. The seemingly raw, but slightly tempered oyster was served with a spoonful of intensely green soup with a chlorophyll-rich, almost metallic taste of wild herbs. Small clouds of white foam and a few pieces of crystal-clear gel made of water from the chilly January sea gave a refreshing contrast to the soup. A few toasted pine nuts added crunch and a smoky taste to the oyster. The humble white, green and grey dish was finished with sprigs of wild herbs and flowers from Collio.

## P.87 — Iñaki Aizpitarte: Raw peasant soup en chabrot

Greens, lardo di Colonnata, bread, local herbs from Il Giardino Commestibile. Aizpitarte played on the winter theme of eating simple dishes prepared from whatever is available. As the ultimate Paris bistronome, he followed the old French country custom called en chabrot — adding wine to the soup bowl at the table. Aizpitarte's soup of foraged herbs and greens was rich in colour and flavour. On this he placed croutons of country bread and added a generous splash of wine from the producer Radikon. He covered the bread with slices of aromatic cured fat from Colonnata and warmed it slightly, giving it an almost translucent shine.

## P.88 — Petter Nilsson:  Where the wild boars are

Jerusalem artichoke, salsify and black truffle. Nilsson, the Swedish chef from restaurant La Gazzetta in Paris, made a dish by literally digging into the soil of the Collio hills. He drew his inspiration from the winter diet of the Friulian wild boar, mainly tubers and roots, and created a dish based on this. On top of a split Jerusalem artichoke lay a stick of rustic, unpeeled salsify, as if left on the ground by a careless wild boar. The taste of the slightly bitter, fibrous tubers was freshened by a sweet and sour apple sauce and spiced up by the peppery aromas of grated wild horseradish and a generous shaving of local black truffle.

## P.89 — Yoshihiro Narisawa: Evolve with the forest

Venison, fruit, honey, nuts, chestnut, vinegar, tree shoots and buds. Chef Narisawa had made elaborate preparations for his poetic interpretation of the forests of Collio. On top of a rustic piece of wood lay a twig with budding shoots, wrapped in thin slices of slightly dried venison, to be chewed from the twig. The twig was decorated with an edible array of fruit, nuts and buds, creating the harmonious effect of a Japanese Ikebana flower arrangement. A hollowed out chestnut was filled with a clear, fragrant infusion of cedar tree to be savoured from the shell.

## P.90 — Daniel Patterson: Imagining Collio from California

Sheep`s milk ricotta, hay gelatine, beet, radish, local herbs from Il Giardino Commestibile. Patterson chose seven different wild herbs provided by farmer-forager Giusy Foschia's Il Giardino Commestibile in the hills just north of Udine. As the title of the dish reveals, Patterson had planned the dish at home and decided to present the best of locally foraged greens combined with some fresh Italian cheese. Slices of crispy red radishes and the wild herbs were arranged with a dramatically red beetroot sauce brushed on one side of the plate. On top of this lay dollops of creamy, rich sheep's milk ricotta.

## P.91 — Pascal Barbot: Moments of joy

Spiny artichoke, pomelo, rose of Gorizia chicory, walnut, garlic and Parmesan. Barbot portrayed his view of the Friulian winter in a dish with local winter vegetables: artichokes and chicory. But among this sombre, cold-weather produce Barbot wanted to include some flavours of the sun: tiny pieces of pomelo added a taste that was simultaneously fresh, sour and sweet. As a familiar and comforting detail Barbot finished the dish with a spoonful of pesto concocted from the three ingredients known to be in every local Italian kitchen cupboard: garlic, walnuts and Parmesan.

### P.92 – David Chang: 40 north, 120 west

Rosa of Gorizia chicory, turnip, kimchi, chestnut, chilli pepper, prosciutto. New York chef Chang imagined his Korean ancestors settling in northeast Italy instead of the USA and asked himself what they would have eaten. He used some methods and local ingredients also used in his restaurants. A small head of local chicory, spiced up with medium-hot kimchi flavours, was contrasted by a creamy chestnut puree. Fermented and pickled baby turnips with wilted stalks provided soft and crisp textures and well-balanced flavours. Chang revealed his admiration of the locally cured ham by adding a few strands of dried prosciutto to the vegetables.

### P.93 – Claude Bosi: Brass monkeys

Pig`s blood, pig`s liver, clams, potatoes and herbs from Il Giardino Commestibile. During the event a pig was slaughtered at a Collio vineyard and some of the meat was served at the following lunch. Bosi drew inspiration from the slaughter and created a theme around the pig's blood, most familiar to him in his home town of Lyon. The fresh blood was mixed with cream to make an uncooked sauce and served with pickled cockles from the Grado lagoon. To this surprising but subtle combination pieces of ash-baked potato and pig's liver parfait were added.

### P.94 – René Redzepi: The Jensen`s hard winter of 1941

Pickled root vegetables, rose petals, elderflowers, sprouts and shoots. Though the produce Redzepi used was Friulian, the dish itself was based on a moment in Danish history. He was inspired by the ordinary, typical Dane, 'Jensen', and his struggle to find food during the severely cold wartime winter of 1941. As the supply of meat, potatoes and produce in general was scarce, the Danes had to find other food sources in their gardens, the forests and the sea. Redzepi's dish was based on several different types of onion, bitter radicchio, foraged herbs and sweet rose petals. The result, presented on a thick slab of grey stone, showed the true potential in produce we too often neglect.

### P.95 – Albert Adrià: Apple rose with an ice cream heart.

The dessert at this dinner was, not surprisingly, handed over to Adrià. He created a seemingly simple but beautiful little gem of a yellow rose which he described as an homage to the rosa of Gorizia – the local chicory. Adrià admitted that it was a demanding dessert to make, consisting of two different textures in need of perfect timing. The juicy, delicate outer petals were crafted from a cocktail of apple juice and sweet wine, while the frozen white heart was made of creamy yogurt and lemon. The rose was finished with a few dewdrops of apple liqueur.

### P.96 – Davide Scabin: The dynamics of ox and hen

Beef broth, egg yolk, truffle and beef glaze. Playing on his home ground, Scabin once more surprised the dinner guests and his chef colleagues. The ox, named Horatio, was slaughtered and 165 lb (75 kilograms) of the meat boiled down to a concentrated, sticky glaze. Scabin then lined the insides of champagne glasses with stripes of this glaze. The hen was represented by an egg yolk in each glass. Hot broth was poured into the glass, and the guests were asked to sip the liquid, then swirl their glass to release more of the meat glaze and repeat the procedure.

AP: Lots of the chefs who attend Cook It Raw feel more creative at the events than they do in their own kitchen. Do you agree?

AA: It's understandable that you think harder at Cook It Raw because you're in an environment where you're surrounded by top chefs; an unfamiliar, challenging environment. Of course we've all got our own egos. We want to stay well ahead of our fellow chefs, and well ahead of the people who are going to be eating. This automatically drives us to reflect more deeply. And reflection is what makes us change. When you're devoted to creativity – which all of us who attend Raw are – then there's a more direct exchange of ideas. For example, I am particularly interested in how cooks perceive their profession. So getting to know more about that, getting to know others – that makes me change my own outlook.

Seeing how these chefs work, and seeing the passion with which they talk about cooking makes you realise why they are where they are and doing what they are doing. And you feel proud to be a part of it. You don't get the opportunity to learn these things at most conferences – they're just rammed with people. I got more out of the four Cook It Raw events than any other events I've ever been to because, with most events, chefs will go along and they'll insist on having their three helpers or they won't go at all. At Cook It Raw, I go and I cook myself, and all of us lend each other a hand.

AP: You said that Cook It Raw changed your cooking style slightly. How so?

AA: I suppose it's represented in a few little ways. I love talking to people and discussing what I'm planning to do, what I'm going to change and that sort of thing.

There's also the fact that, despite it being so short, your mind is firmly engaged in what's going on around you. You discover new ingredients, you see new things, you don't stop eating, asking, tasting. More than anything it is about confronting fear. Fear makes you develop. It is crucial to the creative process.

AP: Fear of failure?

AA: Yes. I am personally extremely affected by the fear of disappointing people who are expecting something of you. When you have to confront something that you have no control over. When it comes to Cook It Raw, you don't approach it feeling that you have to create something new – that goes without saying. You approach it feeling the pressure that comes with cooking for people who expect something of you because of your reputation.

Cooking is nothing more than waking up every morning and asking yourself 'what can I do better? What can I change?' This attitude of continuous self-reflection is so important. Personally, Cook It Raw compels me from the moment I get on the plane. It's like there's a switch in me – part of my brain is plugged in to the event. And this fear feeds my creativity.

AP: It's also a platform for exchanging ideas, for sharing things and getting stimulation from each other?

AA: Of course, of course. Especially bearing in mind that those of us who attend are doing pretty well. And we might not get the chance to spend time together otherwise. It's about surrounding yourself with talented people and having the luxury of time. With that, you can be creative. Cooking is an attitude. Cooking is not about recipe books. Cook it Raw is the same, we feed off each other's talent and enthusiasm. Our creativity is heightened just by all being together.

AP: At every Cook It Raw there was a question you had to address and a new environment to confront. Can you explain how you got your creative juices flowing?

AA: Whenever I cook anywhere I love mixing Spanish ingredients with whatever I'm making. For the four Cook It Raw events I always tried to add an extra little Spanish detail. In Collio I remember that Andrea Petrini sent us an email with a few local ingredients, and out of these the rosa di Gorizia really stood out from the others. Once I had settled on the idea of the rose, I began reflecting on the dryness, the cold, the frost that make up Collio's winter landscape. I wondered how to make a dessert that reflected these elements. Also, for me it is very important that the dish tastes nice – rather than just pushing creative boundaries. Especially when there are so many important guests. So I decided to use apple and to make the dish rather monochromatic, evoking that dryness, that aridity, but making something that tasted very joyful, very interesting.

AP: What does creativity mean to you?

AA: Everybody has a different understanding of what creativity is. I am lucky to be one of the few who gets paid to be creative, rather than to just cook. In this sense, I suppose I approach creativity a bit differently. At elBulli our creativity was a mark of identity – if you went to elBulli, you knew you would get to try out lots of new things.

AP: How did that come about?

AA: In 1997 elBulli was awarded its third Michelin star and that changed things. We dedicated more time to simply being creative.

Ferran decided that he no longer wanted to do variations on existing dishes, but wanted to create things that were entirely new. This was because people were coming from increasingly far and wide and their expectations were getting ever higher. We never looked at what other chefs were doing, because in those days it wasn't that easy to find out. We spent hours and hours reading and studying, and in this way we started learning about how to be creative. It was a completely revolutionary and anarchic approach.

At first we made the mistake of trying to come up with complete dishes. This was a mistake, as a dish can never really be finished. You've got to build the chassis and make the engine, and then tinker around with it in the assembly line. It is only after you give a dish to a customer that it starts taking shape, slowly but surely.

Eventually we started trying out new techniques with water – it dawned on us that water has a neutral pH level, so if an idea doesn't go well with water, then it's not going to go with anything. Our first experiment was around the theme of hot jelly. Ferran had envisaged that making a hot aspic would open up a whole world of creative possibilities. And it did. I remember perfectly how we came up with a very basic form of hot jelly: we started with some strands of seaweed to form a kind of base. This gave us wings and lots of other things sprung from it.

After this success, Ferran said 'let's make our creativity official – let's set up a research & development department'. So we bought premises, spent two years working on the site, and then moved the workshop there in 2001. We grew from two to five people and our creative approach became more and more professional. Our intention was to start afresh every year, which was totally crazy because not only were we having to develop new techniques all the time, but also new dishes, new ways of presenting them and serving them... everything! We changed everything we possibly could with the money we had. And we had to be really fast because we only had six months between September and March in which we could change everything.

So, in terms of developing my creativity, I devoted 10 years – between 1998 and 2008 – to working on it. During that time it became clear that I had the facility to spot something new, something that hadn't been seen before. Getting to this stage has taken thousands and thousands of hours of trial and error – in my head I've got a whole archive, and lots of support too. You've got to surround yourself with well-drilled people.

AP: Is creativity more important than technical ability?

AA: The most important thing for me is that there is a relationship and an understanding between the party giving and the party receiving. In other words, if I'm cooking pizzas, what are the customer's expectations? Technique and creativity both come into this, but first and foremost it's about the quality of the ingredients. I can't make a decent pizza without good tomatoes, good cheese, good flour and good dough. Then comes technique. This is what ensures that your pizza will be different to other pizzas. If you were to go to two pizzerias, you would get two different pizzas. That's the magic of cooking.

Creativity is at the service of technical ability, but is itself at the service of quality ingredients. It's a fiction that modern, avant-garde cooking is all about powders, water baths and aromas. Places like Noma, Mugaritz and Roca all get the best ingredients because they know that is where great cooking begins.

AP: Does technical know-how also help drive creativity?

AA: It's vital. My technique was developed in my early days as a pastry chef, where there's no end to the obstacles you come up against. It's hard to explain. It's like art. You can't treat it like it's not a big deal – you need an attitude that questions everything when you're cooking. You can never quite be happy. What is creativity? Ninety minutes of hell on earth followed one orgasmic minute that you couldn't describe or share with anyone. That inner joy when you make something, when you create something. It's indescribable.

AP: So what is your creative process like?

AA: I have different channels. The first is starting with a blank canvas, which is the most difficult thing. Forgetting about everything you already know. Sitting down and trying to visualise something new. Then there's the way of doing it by association. Saying 'right, I saw this thing being done in such and such a place'. Mimicry. Putting two and two together. This is where technique comes into play. 'How am I going to replicate this dish?' I approach it, I learn it and then I do it my own way. So many factors come into play. Finally, there's a more analytical approach. Looking at books, thinking about things like essence and purity, that's when you find balance and knowledge.

AP: And surely you need time to develop your creativity?

AA: Well, I think it is innate. It's not something that you can learn. You can look for formulae that will take your learning to a certain level, but there's a limit to how far that'll take you.

AP: Creativity is an attitude, too, right? A way of understanding things?

AA: There are some people who talk lightly about creativity. But you must be careful to understand that there are limits to creativity in terms of how demanding it can be. In other words, you can keep yourself within a boundary. Like any artist. You can develop a style and stick to it for your whole life, or you can choose to play around with different styles, and that's what makes you truly great. I think that when you cook and you use different styles you develop a maturity that makes you great.

I remember one night very clearly which was the most creative I have ever felt. It was the day I invented 'Chocolate Earth'. It marked the first time that I had designed something that had been in my head and worked out 100 per cent. I was thinking 'this cannot fail!' It was so obvious! I couldn't sleep after that epiphany. That was in 2003. Now everybody's doing earth and landscapes and that sort of thing and it all stems from that moment, from that night where I woke up at 3am to do some drawings. I folded them up and put them in my bag and rushed to show Ferran the next day – I felt this amazing, childlike excitement!

AP: So it takes time to be creative?

AA: Calmness. The biggest hamper to creativity is the feeling of being contaminated. You need to switch off your phone and surround yourself with talented people. Cooks tend to seek out regularity, which is a mistake. Cook It Raw upsets your regular rhythm and takes away the control of the situation. You need to be shaken up occasionally, without it you'd be lost.

AP: Is this a key to helping you be more creative?

AA: The thing is that sometimes being creative means doing absolutely nothing. I've got my idol, my 'doing nothing maestro', who's this guy in Roses who has a grill and doesn't cook anything fancy. That's the beauty of it. He cooks simple fish and doesn't need to do anything else. He says 'if there's no fish caught locally today, then I'm not opening'. Just fish. He doesn't need salad, he doesn't need potatoes, he doesn't need anything. The tourists say 'he doesn't even have potatoes!' But trust me, eating his food is heavenly. Why would you want potatoes?

AP: What do you take away from each Cook It Raw? What keeps you going back?

AA: Well, first and foremost, the fact that they are such complete experiences. They are so immersive and you really feel like a cook. I think they are the best events I've ever taken part in my life. And I've taken part in many. But I've never seen anything else like Cook It Raw – everybody concentrates so hard and there isn't a beer to be seen until the cooking is finished. Everybody supports each other so much and this has the effect of making you more creative with your work, and when you come back you tell everyone about how well it went, how positive the experience was... Because before you go it is hard to explain what it is exactly.

This is why I love travelling and discovering things. There are a lot of surprises. You think that a certain cuisine is one way, but it's not. You think that a certain person is one way, but they're not. Or you can find yourself confirming what you previously thought — take the north of Italy, for example, where you might suppose that the people are privileged and possessed of a tremendous cultural richness and understanding, right? But in reality it was far simpler, far more pure than that. Remember those breakfasts on the hillside? You're there thinking 'these people know how to live. They just know'. So many great experiences.

# Cook It Raw (III)

## THE DINNERS:

**(I)** Denmark
**NATURE**
Zero energy cooking

Cook It Raw's inaugural dinner in Copenhagen sees the chefs explore nature through a zero energy cooking challenge.

**(III)** Finland
**COLLABORATION**
Cooking in the wild

Cook It Raw heads into the Lappish wilds to test the strength of the brotherhood by holding a collaborative dinner.

**(II)** Italy
**CREATIVITY**
Chef versus winter

During the depths of a Collio winter Cook It Raw's chefs prepare dinner in an experiment of creativity.

**(IV)** Japan
**FUTURE**
Avant-garde meets tradition

The chefs meet the producers and craftsmen of Ishikawa to create a Cook It Raw dinner that marries avant-garde cooking with tradition.

## THE PRINCIPLES:

(I) Nature rules
(II) Limitations boost creativity

(III) Collaboration not competition
(IV) Look back to look forward

## THE CHEFS:

| | | |
|---|---|---|
| ✗ | Albert Adrià | ES |
| ✗ | Iñaki Aizpitarte | FR |
| ✗ | Alex Atala | BR |
| ✗ | Fredrik Andersson | SE |
| ✗ | Pascal Barbot | FR |
| ○ | Mark Best | AU |
| ✗ | Claude Bosi | UK |
| ✗ | Massimo Bottura | IT |
| ○ | Sean Brock | US |
| ✗ | David Chang | US |
| ○ | Mauro Colagreco | AR |
| ✗ | Quique Dacosta | ES |
| ○ | Alexandre Gauthier | FR |
| ○ | Ichiro Kubota | JP |
| ✗ | Yoshihiro Narisawa | JP |
| ✗ | Magnus Nilsson | SE |
| ✗ | Petter Nilsson | SE |
| ✗ | Daniel Patterson | US |
| ✗ | René Redzepi | DK |
| ✗ | Davide Scabin | IT |
| ○ | Ben Shewry | XX |
| ○ | Kondo Takahiko | JP |
| ○ | Yoji Tokuyoshi | JP |
| ✗ | Hans Välimäki | FI |
| ○ | Joachim Wissler | DE |

The chefs travel to the province of Lapland in the far north of Finland for the third instalment of Cook It Raw. Experiencing temperatures below 0°C they get a taste of life in the Arctic Circle and learn about the importance of teamwork to the Sámi people's survival. To test the strength of their brotherhood the chefs are challenged to collaborate on a dinner spanning two evenings.

Area:
8,262.67 km²

Population, Persons:
6,281

Population Density:
Persons per km²
0.78

(A)
Helsinki:
Where the group
boarded the night
train to Lapland

(B)
Levi:
Where the group
stayed

(C)
Lake Jeris:
Where the group
went fishing and
foraging

(D)
Skylight:
Where the final
meal was held

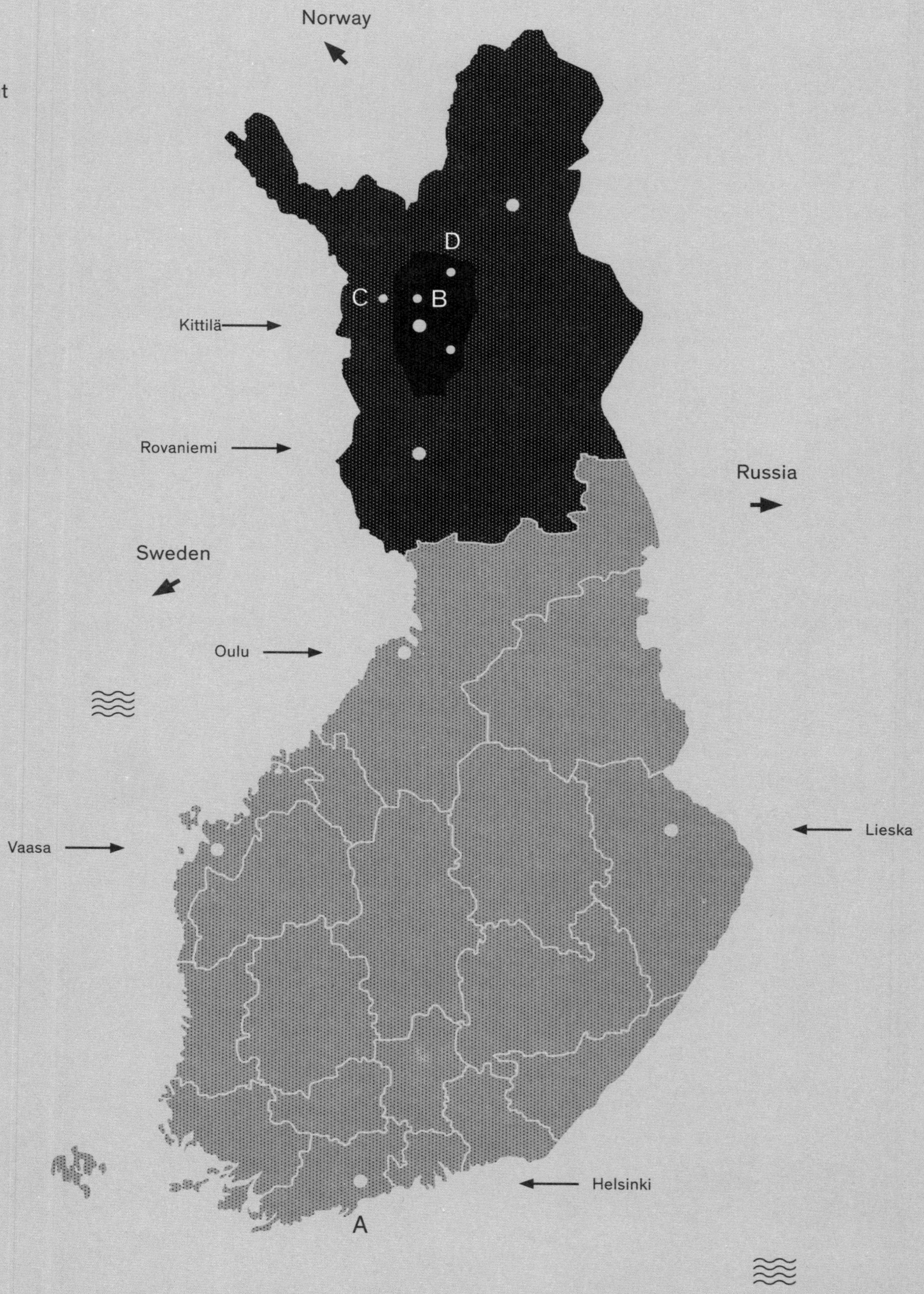

Norway

D

C  B

Kittilä

Rovaniemi

Russia

Sweden

Oulu

Vaasa

Lieska

Helsinki

A

## Raw Ingredients

The Kittilian countryside is Cook It Raw's larder. Deep into the Autumn the following ingredients are available to the chefs to forage:

**Meat:**
Reindeer
Bear
Moose
Goat
Wild mallard duck
Wild hare

**Fish:**
White fish and roe
Vendace and roe
Arctic char
Wild salmon
Pike
Perch
Roach
Noble crayfish

**Berries:**
Blueberries
Lingonberries
Cloudberries
Buckthorns
Rowanberries
Currants
Raspberries
Strawberries
Juniper berries

**Mushrooms:**
Boletus mushrooms
ceps

**Root vegetables:**
Carrots

Turnips
Swedes
Onions
Puikula potatoes

**Forest stuff:**
Sap, buds, moss,
leaves, needles,
lichen, river & lake
reeds, Hays etc.

**Dairy:**
Cow's milk
Reindeer milk
Goat's milk

## The Development of Total Number of Reindeer in Finland

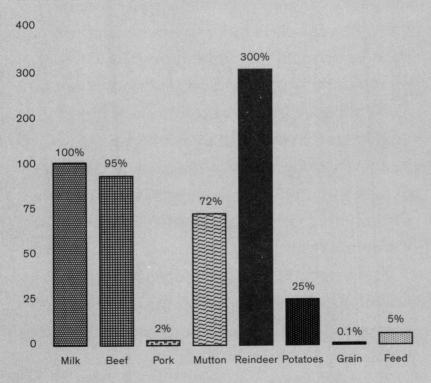

## Lapland's Self-sufficiency in Foodstuffs (%)

## Sami Population

Altogether there are around 70,000 (approx.) Sami in four countries:

Finland:  6,000
Norway: 42,000
Sweden: 20,000
Russia: 2,000

For at least 5000 years the Sami, have occupied Finland, Sweden and Norway.  While their numbers are decreasing and their lifestyles changing the Sami of Lapland still place huge importance on the reindeer. Cook It Raw's chefs witness the slaughter of a reindeer the traditional way and this and other local food ways inspire the chefs preparations for dinner.

The prospect of Lapland lay before us, of crossing the Arctic Circle for the first time in our lives and subsisting there on whatever twigs and berries the frozen tundra might offer, supplemented perhaps by the flesh of a hapless bear or walrus that had wandered into our camp. This would be the fabled land of the midnight sun and the Northern Lights, and herds of wild reindeer.

We assembled shortly before midnight on 3 September 2011 in Helsinki, under the massive arches of the Central Railway Station. The night train to Lapland was waiting on a distant platform, which we had yet to find.

Our group consisted of sixteen celebrated young avant-garde chefs and an equal number of journalists, nearly all based in Europe. We were supervised and well cared for by our two leaders, Alessandro and Andrea, who supplied delectable sandwiches of salmon rillettes and dilled cucumber on dark rye bread, and cured whitefish with crayfish butter on thick slices of wholewheat. Several icy bottles of a Finnish vodka called Koskenkorva magically materialized – the purest and cleanest vodka I have ever tasted, only seventy-five degrees proof but powerfully brain-enhancing and mood-improving. Koskenkorva is possibly a miracle drug.

By the time we pulled out of the station, my wife Caron had transformed our narrow, utilitarian compartment into a snug and sheltering nest. While we slept, our train silently slipped over the Arctic Circle.

Why had we agreed to subject ourselves to the privations of the frozen north? In 2009 a project was born and it was called Cook It Raw. A dozen of Europe's cutting-edge chefs and two Americans, many of them very young, gathered in Copenhagen at Noma, then rated the third best restaurant in the world and later number one. Noma is the creation of René Redzepi, the most prominent proponent of what has come to be known as the New Nordic cuisine. More than any other chef, René began to seek out ingredients that are found only in the wild, cannot be ordered from a supplier, and must be foraged for. Some grow or swim only on the outer fringes of Scandinavia and are not likely to be familiar to any of the restaurant's customers. On that first expedition, René took the visiting chefs to the local woods and beaches and tiny farms where his raw materials come from, then turned over his staff and kitchen to them.

The second time around, in 2010, the Cook It Raw cast was largely the same but the scene shifted to Collio in northeast Italy, near the border of Slovenia. And this year we were among the Lappish people, many of whom, we were told, still live off the land and on the lakes. The expedition was subtitled 'Into the Wild'. In a departure from the previous two events, this time the chefs would work in pairs or small groups. They were not to bring ingredients and recipes, but were expected to forage and improvise. Was it not over-optimistic to expect a dozen successful chefs to follow instructions?

Our thirteen-hour journey came to an end in the town of Kolari, where buses were waiting to drive us to a local ski resort called Levi Spirit. In a few months the ground would be covered with snow six feet (two metres) deep, but this was the beginning of September. Now there was no snow, and the temperature rarely dipped below freezing.

The land was mostly flat, carpeted with forests and dotted with countless lakes and occasional clusters of small wooden buildings. Lapland is not a country but a region comprising those parts of Sweden, Norway and Finland that lie north of the Arctic Circle, plus the Kola peninsula in Russia. But that doesn't mean that the climate is Arctic. Most of Lapland is sub Arctic, just like much of Alaska, Siberia, Canada and northern Mongolia, where the tundra isn't frozen and the glaciers are farther to the north. And so my preconceptions about Lapland could not have been further from the truth, with one exception: on our last evening we were indeed dazzled by the Northern Lights, which took the form of vast, diffuse, translucent green clouds in the dark night sky.

The true Scandinavian languages of Swedish, Danish and Norwegian are considered Germanic and are mutually intelligible. But Finnish belongs to the Balto-Uralic group and so contains very few words that relate to the more familiar European languages. Foreigners are therefore completely mystified by Finnish much of the time, unless they live in Estonia or Latvia, a short distance across the Baltic.

Lapland is the home of the Lapps, a term that is now considered politically incorrect for reasons I hope some day to fathom. Instead, the adjective 'Lappish' is commonly used and regarded as perfectly respectable. Our temporary Lappish home consisted of ten villas in a boundless forest of pine and spruce; the forest floor was covered with tiny plants, leaves, mosses and lichens, an Eden-like scene I had known only in my dreams. The villas were handsome examples of contemporary Finnish design, all wood and glass and concrete; each had a spacious living room and kitchen, three or four bedrooms and a sauna – all in the heart of the vast Lappish wilderness.

On our first night there Timo Nieminen, the executive chef of a local restaurant group, put together a lavish spread for us, laid out on a long table in the villa that was our expedition headquarters. There were thin slices of smoked, roast reindeer; smoked vendace (a type of whitefish) from Lake Mieko; wild morels and other mushrooms; and smoked reindeer pie; organic Lappish eggs; lingonberry bread, which I have tried to replicate back in Manhattan, without perfect success, and a flat white potato bread; Lappish cheese with beetroot (beet) shoots; and Puikula potatoes with pickled cucumbers, leaving me to wonder what Puikula means. Timo considers them the best potatoes in the world.

The next morning, we all gathered on the shores of a cold and misty lake and joined fishermen in motorboats casting their nets and harvesting a good number of smallish – ten-inch (twenty-five-centimetre) – floppy white fish, a staple of their diet. And then we were shown the range of other Lappish ingredients: reindeer meat, bear, white snow grouse (which I had heard are the most delectable of all grouse), which were spread out on the grass alongside the lake. There were white plastic trays of wild berries – golden cloudberries, blueberries and scarlet lingonberries (just three of the fifty berries native to Lapland, thirty-five of which are edible and fifteen poisonous) – and the brilliant orange roe of two varieties of white fish. There were root vegetables, a favourite food in Lapland. And there was reindeer milk – rare and expensive because, we were told, the female reindeer gives very little milk. To those of us who weren't squeamish, the milk was a pleasure to drink; to those who were, I recommended that they switch to a profession other than chef or food writer. And there were amazing mushrooms. The chefs in our group walked inland from the shore, keeping their eyes steadily trained on the ground, and returned a half-hour later with

an abundance of local fungi. One brought back a pair of robust, picture-book Amanita muscarias, five inches (twelve centimetres) high and with a hemispherical cap of the most intense red speckled with white bumps. These are the world-famous psychedelic mushrooms associated with a variety of shamanistic religions, notably in Siberia and Scandinavia, whose holy men, in a trance-like state brought on by ingesting the mushroom, gain access to the spirit world. For reasons either benign or hostile, our two perfect examples of Amanita muscaria were taken away from us. The reason stated was that they were poisonous. Where are the sixties now that we need them?

The average Laplander is ethnically identical to the inhabitants of the more urbanized areas of southern Finland and is not, from what I could tell, eager to embark upon ecstatic voyages to the spirit world. But as you travel north into the wilder, colder, more sparsely populated regions you encounter the Sámi people, the aboriginal Laplanders whose religion combines their native shamanism and animism (a belief in the spirits that reside in animals, plants, rocks and so forth) with Lutheranism from the south. In the traditional Sámi view of the world, humans (both shamans and others) can easily trade places with animals and vice versa, though the barrier between men and women is more difficult to cross. You can say that again. There are reports that when Sámi shamans enter a trance with the help of psychedelic mushrooms, their spirits leave their bodies and travel for great distances; then, when they return home, they fly down the chimney hole in the roof of their yurts (felt tents). This may be the model for the story of St. Nicholas or Father Christmas. The traditional Finnish image of him, however, is positively frightening: he has the head of a goat, is hostile to children and demands gifts from them rather than giving them.

The reindeer that the Sámi find so indispensable for food, clothing and shelter, tools and transport, are a variety of caribou. In Lapland they are not wild but, in a sense, farmed. They roam free, 120,000 of them, throughout Lapland until rounded up late in the year. All the animals are branded with a cut taken from their ears; at the round-up that year's calves are branded in line with the brand of their mother – identified as the female reindeer they stick close to. That's also the time of year when reindeer are slaughtered for their meat, which is then often smoked and frozen.

The bear meat and snow grouse we were shown were both frozen, because it was the close season for hunting them. The reindeer meat too was frozen, but for our edification and for the chefs' menus, one reindeer was slaughtered while we watched, some months earlier than he ordinarily would have been. The killing was humane – a single bullet to the head – and the butchering was clean and quick. But I wondered whether eating reindeer yields enough pleasure to justify killing. In response, both Timo and Heston Blumenthal have told me that fresh reindeer meat can be delicious. On a trip to Siberia for his BBC television series, Heston especially relished the heart, kidneys and liver; Timo grows rhapsodic about rare-roasted loin. 'You can taste the forest,' he says.

Our twelve chefs were strict locavores at the climactic dinners they prepared on our final two nights. Massimo Bottura cooked reindeer tongues sous-vide in plastic bags packed with thyme and mushrooms for twenty hours. Reluctant to leave his sous-vide set-up in a public place, exposed to accident and, yes, even sabotage, Massimo took it into his bathroom where he could protect it all night long.

At the first dinner, David Chang was paired with Petter Nilsson from La Gazzetta in Paris for a dish that never went out to diners: potatoes cooked with spruce and the liver of the reindeer that we had seen slaughtered. For the second dinner, David assisted Davide Scabin who cooked local Arctic char and trout buried in the ground in moss with hot, smoked oil; the fish were served on an elaborate still-life composed of the plants we had seen all around us. The three-Michelin-star Parisian chef Pascal Barbot created a not completely feral but nevertheless delicious dish of hare tartare and a mushroom cream with wild herbs and flowers, after which he whipped up a sauce (or condiment) for Massimo's reindeer tongues from a brunoise of root vegetables, raw fish eggs and sautéed bread. René Redzepi helped Claude Bosi and Magnus Nilsson, who made a stock of many mosses and lichens served with roasted carrots, salt-baked potatoes, and a variety of condiments. At his restaurant in northern Sweden, Fäviken Magasinet and open only in the summer, Magnus cooks wild food entirely by himself for nine guests at a time. René considers him a major young talent.

And then, at our final dinner, just as the Northern Lights were warming up for their midnight performance, Yoshihiro Narisawa created the most powerful dish of our entire expedition. It was highly emotional and delicious at the same time – in the conventional sense of engendering simple pleasure, rarely a primary goal in avant-garde or modernist cooking. Narisawa rounded up every type of animal protein the chefs had been given – reindeer meat, frozen bear and snow grouse – which seemed closer to the Lappish diet than the vegetable-based dishes of other chefs. From these he concocted the deepest, darkest possible broth. This was poured over roots, berries and mosses in large, white, steeply angled bowls. And the bowls had been splattered and splashed with shocking crimson berry juice that recalled the blood of the young reindeer whose slaughter we had all been part of and that had disturbed so many of us, including Narisawa.

So what is the native diet of Lapland? First of all, who are the natives? Someone born in Lapland who never leaves it for very long is considered a native, but beyond this there is fierce controversy. Timo, for example, was born in Lapland in 1970 to non-Lappish parents who soon moved to another part of Finland. In 1998 he came back to stay, taking a job as head chef in the Sirkantähti Hotel in Levi. He has been told by some Laplanders that he is not a genuine Laplander. By this standard, there must be very few true Laplanders in Lapland besides the Sámi people.

Some residents of Lapland dine in a cosmopolitan manner. A twenty-year-old Laplander who was babysitting for a member of our group told me that she rarely eats reindeer meat and then only in restaurants. And on our local Lappish excursions, we often drove past a little mall that displayed a prominent pizza sign. Although I've met some Laplanders who eat only local food, even the most dedicated among them are not complete locavores. After all, wheat does not grow in Lapland; nor sugar or black pepper. Our chefs were stricter, purer of heart, and I was impressed by their ingenuity. Nonetheless, at our final meeting René criticized some members of the group, unnamed, for resisting the spirit of the hunter-gatherer, the forager. I have no doubt that if the chefs had spent the winter and the following spring in Levi, their ingenuity and especially their great hunger would have motivated them to create a true cutting-edge Lappish haute cuisine.

Night train departs from Helsinki to Kolari – direct train to Lapland.
There are cabins for two and the bunks are big and comfortable.
We will organise a corridor party where you can picnic.

A

B

A   The group gather on the platform at Helsinki, awaiting the train that will take them to Lapland.

B   Claude Bosi settles into his bunk.

Presentation of local produce by Timo and Tero. There will be vegetables, funghi, plants, fish and meat. The produce on display here will be the same items that you will have available to you for the final meal.

A

A  Iñaki Aizpitarte investigates some
wild Lappish mushrooms.

Transfer by bus to the nearby Lake Jerisjärvi. We will fish, hunt, pick berries
and wild plants. The weather may be wet, so wear suitable clothing.
An al fresco lunch will be served.

A

B

C

A  Fish roe is harvested for use in
   Massimo Bottura and Pascal
   Barbot's dish.

B  Fredrik Nilsson inspects a lakeside
   find.

C  The empty ovarian sacks of the
   whitefish after the roe has been
   removed.

D

E

F

D  The unspoilt woodlands around Lake Jerisjärvi make it a perfect foraging ground.

E  Fredrik Andersson and Iñaki Aizpitarte explore Lake Jerisjärvi by boat.

F  A fisherman guts one of the catch in preparation of a simple lunch.

G  One of the fishing guides pulls in a net laden with fish.

H    I

J K

H   David Chang harvests lichens and mosses from the forest floor.

I   Wild blueberries are foraged for René Redzepi, Claude Bosi and Magnus Nilsson's collaborative dish.

J   The autumnal weather has left the ground littered with leaves that are ripe for foraging.

K   Daniel Patterson proffers up his finds for inspection.

L

M

L　Alex Atala celebrates after taking a
　　successful shot.

M　A guide takes to the lake to retrieve
　　one of Atala's kills.

The chefs will witness a reindeer slaughter. All of the meat and produce from the animal will be made available for the chefs to use in their dishes. This will include 4 litres of reindeer milk, the most expensive in the world.

A

B

C

A   The reindeer is skinned. Its hide will be used to make clothing and no part of the animal will be wasted.

B   Reindeer blood is whipped to prevent it from coagulating.

C   The reindeer slaughter is quick and humane, but this does not detract from the brutal reality of the event.

Return to Levi Spirit to prepare for dinner. Shuttles to the evening venue will
depart at 16:00. The dinner commences at 21:00 followed by an afterparty.

A

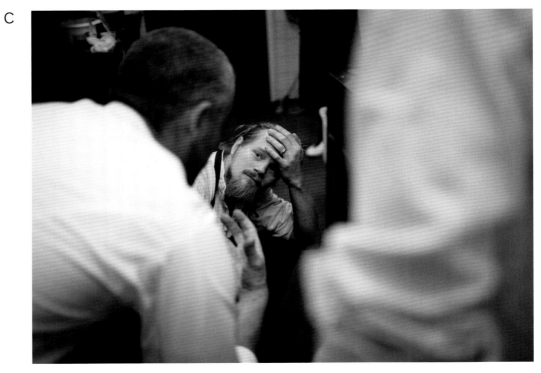

A   Fredrik Andersson, Alex Atala and
Hans Välimäki discuss their
collaborative dish.

B   Daniel Patterson talks Davide Scabin
through his dish.

C   The pressure of collaborative
cooking starts to show on the faces
of Andersson and Atala.

D

E

D   David Chang gets started on his dashi.

E   Davide and David work together on their final dish of Arctic char.

F   Quique Dacosta watches the diners arrive for the final meal.

'You don't come here to learn, but you learn.
You don't come to teach, but you teach.
I think Cook It Raw is distinct and unique.
It's like playing jazz or pop.'

Quique Dacosta

G

H

I

G   Fredrik Andersson prepares the Puikula potatoes for his dish.

H   Alex Atala gets started on making his tortellini.

I   Massimo Bottura takes charge of service.

J   Pascal Barbot starts the delicate process of plating up.

J

K

L

M

K  Albert Adrià and Claude Bosi start
to relax as the diners settle into
their meal.

L  The chefs relax with a glass of wine
after the meal is over.

M  The Northern Lights put on a
stunning show as Cook It Raw Lapland
comes to a close.

Pascal Barbot
A cream of wild mushrooms, hare tartare, lichens and country bread

Fredrik Andersson
Raw Lappish turnip, wild sorrel, dried fish salt, lingonberries and cream

Iñaki Aizpitarte & Petter Nilsson
Vendace, braised beetroot, raw mushrooms, sorrel, reindeer broth, porcini and lichen broth, and lingonberries

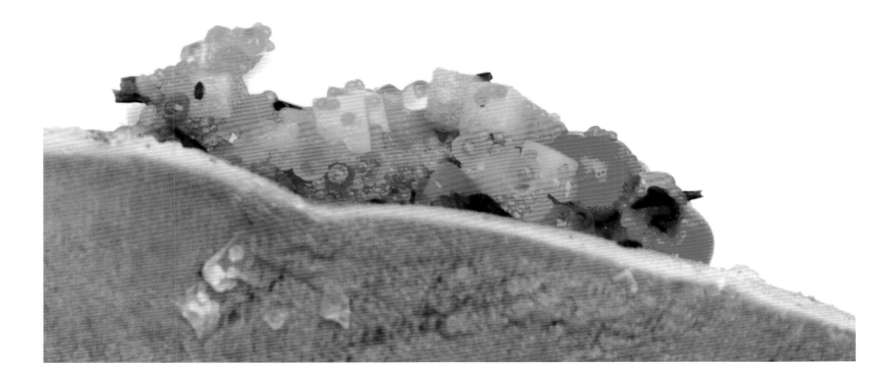

Massimo Bottura & Pascal Barbot
Reindeer tongue, root vegetables and whitefish roe

Massimo Bottura
White risotto, raw wild fish and undergrowth

Albert Àdria
Rye bread ice cream, mushroom and balsamic caramel, yoghurt, apples and honey

Yoshihiro Narisawa
The forest – mushrooms in the undergrowth

Quique Dacosta
The rose and the red snow

Alex Atala, Hans Välimäki & Fredrik Andersson
Tortellini of reindeer blood, reindeer heart, puffed barley and light lingonberry broth

René Redzepi, Magnus Nilsson and Claude Bosi
Carrots, Lappish potatoes, raw wild mushrooms, lingonberries, blueberries and broth

Alex Atala, Hans Välimäki and Fredrik Andersson
Lappish Puikula potatoes and bearnaise with maté

Daniel Patterson
Baked beets, blueberry and beet juice, sorrel and lingonberries

Yoshihiro Narisawa
Life and death

Davide Scabin and David Chang
Arctic char and Lapland dashi with reindeer milk

Albert Adrià
Blood and snow

P.130 – Pascal Barbot:
A cream of wild mushrooms, hare tartare, lichens and country bread

Barbot created a tiny dish that showcased the true tastes of the Lappish forest. From the intensely aromatic and gamey meat of the Lappish wild hare he made a tartare. This was placed on a rich puree of wild

P.132 – Iñaki Aizpitarte and Petter Nilsson: Vendace, braised beetroot, raw mushrooms, sorrel, reindeer broth, porcini and lichen broth, and lingonberries

Two of the most creative bistronome chefs of Paris, Aizpitarte and Nilsson cooked a dish truly representative of their genre with an intense

P.134 – Massimo Bottura:
White risotto, raw wild fish and undergrowth

Bottura wanted to add an Italian touch to one of his dishes. In a huge stockpot by the fireplace in one of the chalets he cooked a white risotto as the warm and rustic element of the dish. On the plate, he added produce typical ...pish undergrowth – ...rooms, blueberries ... flowers – and raw ...hitefish. The hot ...htly cooked the fish, ... contrast between ..., familiar flavours ...ild produce.

...bert Adrià (1st night):
...ice cream, mushroom ...ic caramel, yoghurt, ... honey.

...his workshop with ...d an ice-cream ... an unheated ... a Lappish chalet, ...is hands on two ...nnish breakfast ... the ice cream he ...ead buns and cans ...ogurt. He cooked an ...rup of mushrooms ...ic vinegar and ...lved local apples ... were served with ...ade of honey, ...ed by the yogurt and ...m.

P.136 – Yoshihiro Narisawa:
The forest – mushrooms in the undergrowth

Wild mushrooms baked in a salt crust covered with spruce shoots, juniper and lingonberry plants. Narisawa opened the Cook It Raw dinner with a dramatic dish resembling a piece of smoking Lappish forest. Pieces of smoking and steaming forest vegetation on rustic planks of pine wood were placed on the tables, then cut open with hunting knives to release an intense aroma of wild mushrooms. Whole mushrooms, picked in the forests near Levi, were baked in a shell made of salt and flour crust.

P.137 – Quique Dacosta: The rose and the red snow

Endive, rose, red beet and lichens. Beautiful and a visually dramatic, Dacosta's deep purple-and-red dish consisted of a rose made from an endive. The endive was flavoured with a beet-and-moss infusion and got its bright red colour from the beet juice. To enhance its earthy flavour the beet juice was infused with moss and lichens and beet vinegar was added. The dish got an aroma of rose petals from roses picked at a Lappish lake the day before. With the endive a lightly frozen ice was served, made from the same infused beet juice and a dash of reindeer blood.

# R.S.V.P.

## Raw, *s'il vous plaît*

COOK IT RAW / INTO THE WILD
GALA DINNER

*Lapland, september 6th 2010*

P.138 – Alex Atala, Hans Välimäki and Fredrik Andersson: Tortellini of reindeer blood, reindeer heart, puffed barley and light lingonberry broth

Atala , Välimäki and Andersson decided that they wanted to cook some of the reindeer that had been butchered at a nearby Lappish farm that morning. The most interesting parts they considered to be the blood and the heart. They served tortellini filled with reindeer blood pudding, the pasta made by Atala using Finnish flour. To this, small cubes of reindeer heart were added, and a red broth with lingonberries was poured over.

P.139 – René Redzepi, Magnus Nilsson and Claude Bosi: Carrots, Lappish potatoes, raw wild mushrooms, lingonberries, blueberries and broth

Redzepi, Nilsson and Bosi decided to serve a rustic communal dish. Lappish Puikula potatoes and carrots were baked in clay pots with sea salt and moss. The diners were asked to serve themselves from the pots, then add raw mushrooms to the dish and pour a hot mushroom broth over the lot. The dish was finished with fresh blueberries and lingonberries, as is the custom with several rustic Scandinavian dishes of the Nordic countries. The chefs categorized their dish as Lappish comfort food.

P.140 – Alex Atala, Hans Välimäki, Fredrik Andersson: Lappish Puikula potatoes and bearnaise with maté.

The Puikula potato, a special variety grown only in Lapland, is Välimäki's favourite. The chefs spent the better half of the day tending the potatoes, baked on a piece of slate over a cracked fireplace in an ancient log barn. The sweet, almond-tasting potato flesh was complemented by an airy and refreshingly acidic béarnaise seasoned with the maté herb that Atala had brought with him from Brazil. The dish was served on a piece of rock, with flecks of green and grey lichen growing on it.

P.141 – Daniel Patterson: Baked beets, blueberry and beet juice, sorrel and lingonberries

Much of the wild produce on offer in Lapland was familiar to Patterson from the forests of New England and California, but even so he was amazed by the intense flavours of the wild herbs. As the main ingredient of his dish he used local beets. To enhance their sweet and earthy flavour, he roasted them for several hours in the open fireplace in the lodge. The juice of blueberries and beets was reduced to a thick, red sauce with some reindeer blood. The sauce, together with fresh sorrel leaves and lingonberries were added to the beets.

P.142 – Yoshihiro Narisawa: Life and death

Hare fillet, bear and game consommé, pine shoot syrup, lingonberries and blueberries. Throughout the event, Japanese chef Narisawa was deeply moved by the Lappish wilderness and its wildlife. In an emotional presentation, he explained the message of his dish. Its creation had entailed taking the lives of many wild animals, but the result, a rich, dark consommé, had passed these lives on to the guests in a dish full of flavours and nourishment. Pieces of hare fillet and consommé occupied the centre of each plate, surrounded by were splashes of a blood-red sauce of wild berries, which added an exciting visual touch.

P.143 – Davide Scabin, David Chang: Arctic char and Lapland dashi with reindeer milk

Arctic char, Lapland dashi, mushroom crisp. Scabin had heard of the Finnish tradition of baking lamb in a hot fire pit covered with soil, and decided to use this technique with fish. After fellow chef Hans Välimäki helped him to dig the pit, Scabin covered the Arctic char in shaves of pine bark, spruce branches and wild herbs before wrapping it all in a wet blanket. The parcel was then cooked underground in the soil-covered pit. Aftewards, the fish was served with a bowl of dashi made by Chang, with charred fresh onions, a mushroom crisp and some fresh reindeer milk.

P.144 – Albert Adrià: Blood and snow

Powdery yogurt snow, orange and beet juice, coffee, sesame, peppermint and lingonberries. Ending the long final Cook It Raw dinner, Adrià served a dish fit for the setting in Lapland: a plate of light yogurt snow with a few dashes of blood-red orange and beet juice. The story behind the dish was the idea of being lost for three weeks in the wilderness with a reindeer. At the end, one would kill the reindeer and eat it with snow as the only source of water. To Accompany the dessert, a glass of red juice made of beetroot and orange was served.

18/6/10 12:27AM

By the way, we would like not to do a proper dinner and organize instead two to three groups scouting the grounds, fishing/hunting/picking and 'cooking' collectively inside the apartments like a real workshop, a team pushing the boundaries beyond the singular authorship.
Do you fancy that?

14/8/10 6:24AM

Dan, have you listened carefully to David Sylvian's Manafon (you can download it on his website)? Can you answer back to the questions I sent to you a few days ago and particularly concerning the dramaturgy of this raw which is directly inspired by the instant composing for small ensembles (duos, trios, quartets) recording of this oratorio? Please also read the note, and the introspective theorizing of Sylvian.
A big hug!

14/8/10 10:58PM

One thing about these improvisations: a kitchen is always a little bit an improvisation, a collaboration, especially a modern kitchen. But there's still one director/editor, one final decision. Same with Sylvian, he's still, as he says, 'gently nudging the session'. If we are cooking together, will there be one person in each group doing the 'gentle nudging'? A collaboration of equals can be dangerous. Know what I mean?

It was the summer of 2010, a few months before the third Cook It Raw, which was set to be held in Finland. Raw's creative director, Andrea Petrini, had come up with a new idea for the event that was possibly disastrous and most certainly masochistic. To cook in groups, together, was normal. To jointly create dishes as collaborative teams was not.

It's not like we didn't work well together. Since the first time the chefs met, working together had been a joy. The energy in the kitchen when we were cooking a dinner was special: relaxed, focused, curious, supportive. We had always helped each other, but we had all made our own dishes. To understand the importance of collaboration in modern kitchens, look at elBulli. They changed all the rules about creativity, about sharing and publishing ideas, about working as a team. Now we have pastry chefs making savoury dishes, and savoury chefs making sweet ones. We have lab chefs generating ideas in the same way as do the Research & Development departments of the industrial food industry. We have huge teams of paid chefs along with stages working for free, a group of people all contributing to a shared, collective understanding. But it always starts with one person, one vision.

'Collaboration' might not be the right word for what is special about Cook It Raw. Maybe the right word is 'sharing'. Or 'inspiring'. Certainly 'friendship'. During the first event, we bonded immediately, leaving with connections that deepened over time. We saw each other at food conferences, visited each other's restaurants, shared employees and information about cooking techniques, business practices. But most of all we shared ideas. Not just ideas about how to do our jobs better, but about the changing roles of chefs, about how we can make the world a better place. We saw the others pushing and innovating in their restaurants, and it inspired us to do better ourselves. But we each came with our own distinctive styles, our own voices. And those voices, rather than merging, became more distinctive over time.

Now we were being told to follow a composer and musician named David Syvian, who made the record Manafon. But, the idea for that record did not arise spontaneously. Sylvian created it. We arrived in Lapland still slightly dazed after a vodka-soaked train ride from Helsinki. The resort – normally a destination for the rich and famous – was a small campus of buildings scattered around a forest. Inside, the houses looked like eco-modernist skiing lodges: open floor plans, floor to ceiling windows, vast living areas. The kind of place that was perfect for hanging out and talking late into the night.

We dropped our bags in our rooms and gathered outside. The products we could work with were laid out in boxes on the grass beside one of the houses. There was fish, root vegetables, wild berries and slabs of meat. Photographers snapped pictures while the chefs studied the products. And every one of them was thinking about what they wanted to cook. I wandered off into the forest with Petter Nilsson and Iñaki Aizpitarte to eat wild berries and herbs.

That night we went to Tuikku, a restaurant perched on top of a mountain of green undulating hills that stretched out to the horizon. In between bites of reindeer sausage, reindeer hamburgers and slow-cooked reindeer, we talked about Andrea's idea of cooking in teams.

'Do you think he's serious?', one chef asked.

'Oh yeah,' I said. 'He's serious all right.' We shook our heads and did another shot of cloudberry brandy.

The next morning we visited a nearby lake. Some of the chefs boarded small boats to try their luck at fishing, while others, myself among them, took to the woods. Along the way we found sheep sorrel, and in a nearby garden, flowering coriander (cilantro). There were strawberries with a depth of flavour that was stunning – perhaps the constant sunlight and pristine soil combined to ripen the fruit more slowly and fully. It made me wonder if the root vegetables would have the same sweetness.

After an hour traipsing through the woods, picking lichens, mushrooms and berries, there was a collective realization: we all had basically the same ingredients. The biodiversity of edible plants available to us was not vast and, for some reason, everyone wanted to work with reindeer blood.

As we drove back to our temporary home, I sat next to Yoshihiro Narisawa, whom I had been partnered with, and talked about 'our' dish.

'What do you think about pine mushrooms baked in a dough flavoured with the forest', he asked, showing me the bag of bark, lichens and herbs he brought back.

'Um, sounds good.'

'And maybe we can make a dish with a reindeer and a berry sauce that looks like blood, and a consommé of game, about the killing of the reindeers?'

'Sounds great!' It was becoming pretty clear that my involvement was largely going to consist of nodding and smiling.

On the way back to the chalets, we stopped by Skylight, the house where the dinner would be held. I say house – it might have been

a restaurant, but it was awfully hard to tell. Especially when we saw the kitchen. There were a few banged-up ovens, a small walk-in fridge and out back, a verdant lawn that stretched to a river, a few smoke houses in between, a small garden, patches of herbs and flowers here and there. It was beautiful, rustic, and totally ill-equipped to produce the kind of food that the chefs were used to cooking.

We sat in the dining room around a giant wooden table and divided into teams. Some of the guys were to cook that night in the chalets, because they had to leave early. The rest would cook for the second dinner. René Redzepi was paired with Claude Bosi and Magnus Nilsson. Alex Atala with Fredrik Andersson and Hans Välimäki. David Chang with Davide Scabin. And I was paired with Petter Nilsson and Yoshihiro Narisawa. We discussed who would be using what ingredients, and then separated up into our groups to talk about our dishes.

I looked at the giant fireplace, and thought about something I'd seen the day before. On a walk outside the chalets, the path through the forest passed by an enclosed rock outcropping. Inside, a family sat on rock benches, huddled around a fire that danced in the late afternoon light. A few feet further along the path was a wild juniper bush. And beyond, a sea of wild blueberries.

What if I roasted beets in the open fireplace? This would have the dual benefit of being something I'd never done before, and also it would keep me out of the kitchen for

149

most of the day. A sauce of beetroot (beet) juice, juniper and reindeer blood. Some sheep sorrel. I boarded the bus for the camp thinking about the dish. My dish.

If the kitchen at the event was a disaster, the ones in the chalets, though charming, were even worse. Chefs crammed onto burners too small for their pots, and sprawled out onto dining room and coffee tables to prep.

Claude Bosi, who first met Pascal Barbot in the kitchen at L'Arpege, helped brunoise vegetables for a vinaigrette for Pascal and Massimo Bottura's sous vide reindeer tongue.

'This is amazing,' he said, holding up a picture-perfect cube and laughing, 'I haven't done this in years. Look, I still remember!'

Iñaki Aizpitate and Petter Nilsson had been fishing that morning, and made a stellar dish of vendace, beetroots and mushroom broth scented with lichen. Fredrik Andersson created a dish with raw turnips, sorrel and lingonberries. Massimo, in addition to the reindeer tongue, made risotto. And for dessert, Albert Adrià served rye bread ice cream with wild mushroom caramel, balsamic vinegar and yogurt. Afterwards, we sat around giant fires drinking wine, and then scattered in groups to the chalets, where we talked into the night.

It was early the next morning when we arrived at the Skylight, traces of mist still clinging to the shaggy lawn. We rubbed our eyes sleepily, looking around for our ingredients.

'What's this?' asked René. He had found the two pans of consommé that Narisawa had cooked in the oven overnight. He found a knife and sliced off a piece of meat. We were curious. We were also starving. Feeding the chefs was apparently not part of the program.

I took a bite. It was dark and meaty, rich with a gamey, greasy quality that was halfway between pleasant and unpleasant. It was both vaguely familiar and totally new. It took me all of two seconds to make the connection. René and I looked at each other and said at the same time.

'Bear.' We put the rest of the meat back in the pot.

The early part of the morning involved a lot of shuffling around, looking for pots and pans, and building fires. I was ostensibly working with Petter and Narisawa, but it didn't play out quite like that. Narisawa took Taka (a chef from Osteria Francescana who stayed behind after Massimo Bottura had left), and together they prepped Narisawa's dishes. By this point we'd given up any pretense of my involvement. Petter, who had also cooked the night before, was a little slow out of the gate, and his morning mostly consisted of running his hands through his mussed-up hair and looking for caffeine. I told him what I was working on: beetroots (beets) roasted in front of an open fire; a sauce of beetroot (beet) juice; wild blueberries and juniper, thickened with reindeer blood; sheep sorrel, and something else, to be decided. He nodded in support and agreement, then mussed his hair again and wandered off for a walk around the grounds. When he came back he

150

decided to bake bread and – god bless him – cook lunch for the chefs.

My idea turned out to be more challenging than I thought. I built the fire and put the beetroots (beets) next to it in a metal pan. They sat there, basking in a warm sunshine glow, not cooking. Claude, working on a nearby table, raised his eyebrows.

'You know the dinner is tonight, yeah?' he asked helpfully.

'Yes.'

'There is no way those beetroots are going to be ready.'

'Yes they are.'

'Why don't we make a bet. Dinner at each other's restaurant.' He paused. 'And a plane ticket. Business class.' I looked at the beetroots again. He did have a point. I dumped the beetroots (beets) out onto the bare flagstone and stoked up the fire until it was double the size. I spent most of the next six hours moving beetroots around the fireplace floor. But, in the end, they cooked. They were, in fact, a revelation, juicy, sweet and deeply flavoured. The sauce was sweet, sour, delicately herbaceous and sharpened by the iodine edge of the blood. With the green ping of the sorrel, the dish was almost perfect. Almost. I ate it with Petter, who by now had awakened fully.

'What about lingonberries,' he said.

'I thought of that, but everybody's using them. Fuck it, ok… But in what form?'

'What if we half dry them by the fireplace?' And there it was. Brilliant. The one

perfect finishing touch. The berries would be warm, concentrated, explosively flavoured, a counterpoint to the deep, sweet, earthy beetroots.

Whatever Andrea had planned, in the end it played out pretty much like we all figured. The best dishes were the ones with a singular director. The more collaborative ones ended up somewhere in the middle. And there was one absolute, unmitigated disaster. That was David Chang and Davide Scabin's dish. They couldn't have done more to prove the impossibility of a collaboration of equals if they tried. Because, of course, there are no true equals. David, one of the most respectful chefs I know, ceded decision making to the older Davide. And Davide was set on cooking an Arctic char buried in the ground. The fact that he'd never tried this before did not phase him at all.

'Why would I travel six thousand miles to cook the same dish I can cook in my own restaurant?' he said. He had a point. David took on the supporting role. He decided to make a dashi of forest flavours to go with the salmon. And, just in case, he planned to cook some Arctic char also, poached in oil slowly in one of the nearby smoking houses. It would be, under the best of circumstances, Arctic char in two servings.

It was not, of course, anything close to the best of circumstances. Davide dug a hole and went off to take a nap, leaving David to handle all the prep. He apparently came back well rested, because he found time for an amorous moment with his girlfriend in, of all places, the sauna where David was gently cooking his Arctic char in oil. They found the tent too cold, so they stoked the fire. I'm sure you can see where this is going. This is where the dinner hit some road bumps. Their dish fell behind, as David rushed to prep more salmon to make up for the horribly overcooked first batch. Other dishes consequently had to be moved around at the last minute. And, in the case of the René, Claude and Magnus's dish, some elements that were carefully timed became overcooked and as a result were unservable. Collaboration happens not only within a dish, but also between dishes.

David was a good sport about the whole thing. He added some reindeer milk to his broth and served the dish, just before Davide entered with his Arctic char, which ended up having about as much moisture as the dirt in which it had been cooked. Earth is not exactly a finely tuned cooking medium.

Albert finished the night with a brilliant dish of many flavours buried under a thick coating of yogurt 'snow'. It was beautiful and precise. Moving in unison, like engines behind a caboose, were Albert, Quique and Juan Francisco Valiente, with Luciana pulling up the rear, and occasionally breaking away to sprint back to the kitchen and change the can of yogurt snow. Four dishes by four dishes, they worked quickly and in perfect harmony, Albert leading and the others following in unison.

It was a perfect collaboration.

# Cook It Raw (IV)

## THE DINNERS:

**[I]  Denmark**
**NATURE**
Zero energy cooking

Cook It Raw's inaugural dinner in Copenhagen sees the chefs explore nature through a zero energy cooking challenge.

**[II]  Italy**
**CREATIVITY**
Chef versus winter

During the depths of a Collio winter Cook It Raw's chefs prepare dinner in an experiment of creativity.

**[III]  Finland**
**COLLABORATION**
Cooking in the wild

Cook It Raw heads into the Lappish wilds to test the strength of the brotherhood by holding a collaborative dinner.

**[IV]  Japan**
**FUTURE**
Avant-garde meets tradition

The chefs meet the producers and craftsmen of Ishikawa to create a Cook It Raw dinner that marries avant-garde cooking with tradition.

## THE PRINCIPLES:

[I]  Nature rules
[II]  Limitations boost creativity

[III] Collaboration not competition
[IV] Look back to look forward

## THE CHEFS:

| | | |
|---|---|---|
| ✖ | Albert Adrià | ES |
| ○ | Iñaki Aizpitarte | FR |
| ✖ | Alex Atala | BR |
| ○ | Fredrik Andersson | SE |
| ○ | Pascal Barbot | FR |
| ✖ | Mark Best | AU |
| ✖ | Claude Bosi | UK |
| ○ | Massimo Bottura | IT |
| ✖ | Sean Brock | US |
| ✖ | David Chang | US |
| ✖ | Mauro Colagreco | AR |
| ○ | Quique Dacosta | ES |
| ✖ | Alexandre Gauthier | FR |

| | | |
|---|---|---|
| ○ | Ichiro Kubota | JP |
| ✖ | Yoshihiro Narisawa | JP |
| ✖ | Magnus Nilsson | SE |
| ○ | Petter Nilsson | SE |
| ✖ | Daniel Patterson | US |
| ✖ | René Redzepi | DK |
| ○ | Davide Scabin | IT |
| ✖ | Ben Shewry | XX |
| ✖ | Kondo Takahiko | JP |
| ✖ | Yoji Tokuyoshi | JP |
| ○ | Hans Välimäki | FI |
| ○ | Joachim Wissler | DE |

The fourth edition of Cook It Raw sees the chefs visit Ishikawa prefecture in Japan to explore the role that tradition plays in modern gastronomy. Each chef is paired with a local artisan who creates a special plate, bowl or dish for them to present their food in. Over the course of their stay the chefs are instructed in the ikejime technique for slaughtering fish and try their hands duck hunting using only nets.

Area:
4,185 km²

Population, Persons:
1,166,643

Population Density:
Persons per km²
278.72

Power Consumed:
kWh per household
6,446

(A)
Kano Shuzo sake
distillery in Kaga

(B)
Satoyama Forest:
Where they went
foraging

(C)
Hasidate Port:
Where they went
to a crab auction

(D)
Nano Fish Market:
Where they learnt
how to kill fish the
Japanese way

(E)
Katano Kamoike
Bird Sanctuary,
Katano:
Where they went
duck hunting

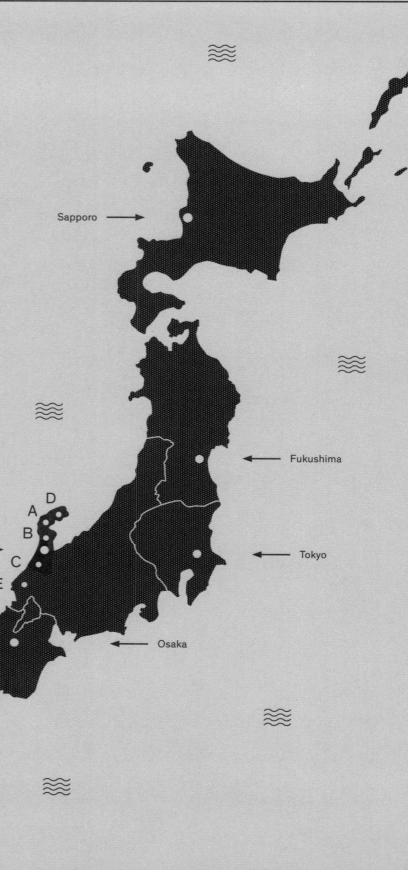

Ingredients for the chef's are foraged, hunted or supplied by local producers. As it's early winter the following ingredients are available:

**Mushrooms:**
Shiba
Oyster
Frost
Shiitake
Shimeji

**Herbs:**
Wasabi
Ginger
Japanese parsley
Lemon balm

**Grains & Beans:**
Rice
Buckwheat

Azuki beans
Ginkgo nuts

**Fruit:**
Pears
Apples
Kaki persimmon

**Meat:**
Noto beef
Duck
Wild boar

**Fish:**
Japanese sea perch
Japanese jack
Mackerel

Tuna
Snow crab
Gasu shrimp
Whelk shell
Noto oyster
Noto sea cucumber

**Vegetables:**
Mustard greens
Okinawa spinach
Nakijima spinach
Crown daisy
Kaga futo kyuri
Cucumber
Taro stem
Japanese yam
Edible burdock

Regions with a high concentration of craftsmen engaged in the creation and production of Japanese traditional arts and crafts:

Ishikawa     Gunma     Tokyo
Kyoto        Fukuoka

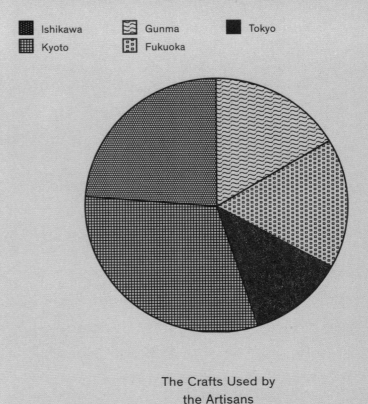

The Crafts Used by
the Artisans

Food Supply
(Kg/Year, per Person)

A list of the crafts used by the artisans:

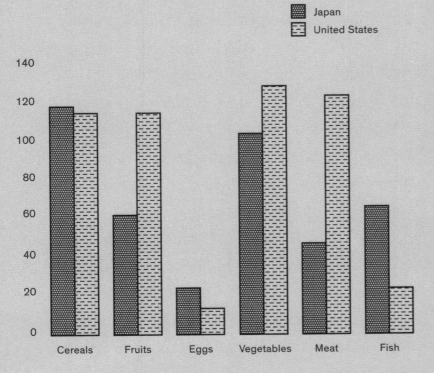

Japan
United States

Glass          Clay
Earthenware    Metal
Lacquerware    Ceramic
Porcelain      Cloth
Paper          Wood

With more traditional crafts produced in Ishikawa prefecture than in any other region in Japan its capital, Kanazawa, was awarded City of Craft status by UNESCO in 2009. Cook It Raw's chefs take their inspiration from the work of local artists their ceramics, lacquerware, silk screen and glasswork acting not only as serving plates for the chef's dishes but as a means of exploring tradition in modern gastronomy.

Early morning, somewhere in Japan. Magnus Nilsson, sitting on a bus, cradling the small figure of a wooden horse in his lap, is noshing on a wasabi and white chocolate Kit Kat. At his side is a basket holding a spade and a wooden-handled scythe. Basket and tools are for collecting the wild-growing findings that Magnus and the other chefs will use to compose their dishes at the dinner that forms the climax of this year's Cook It Raw. (The Kit Kat is a bus snack, an anti-inspiration; the purpose of the wooden horse is never established.)

## THE FORAGE

Typically, Magnus spends two hours every day foraging around Fäviken Magasinet, his remarkable twelve-seat restaurant in northern-middle-of-nowhere Sweden. At home, his routine is solitary – just a chef and his loyal dog. Today he is joined by his colleagues and trailed by a camera crew, intent on getting close-ups of the moment of discovery.

The chefs, their minders and attending journalists have assembled noisily in a field in the foothills of Mount Hakusan. Here they will be split into smaller teams and despatched by bus into the border territory where the farmers' fields end and the true mountains begin.

Despite the made-for-TV feel of the exercise, this is a working mission and the chefs hit the damp forest floor running. Their goal is to fill their baskets with enough weeds, berries, unknown flowers and delicious whatevers to make fifty covers and pull some measure of excitement and taste coherence from an unfamiliar landscape.

'Too small to eat' says Yoshiro Narisawa, tossing a runt of a wasabi rhizome back into the gurgling creek.

Non-Japanese chefs are amazed by the fact that here is wasabi growing in the wild, sprouting plentifully just steps from the path, and that they can grab a handful and chew on its peppery leaves and behold its nubby green root in its raw natural context.

Narisawa pulls up a more impressive specimen, washes it clean in the stream and hands it to Magnus for inspection. The Brazilian chef Alex Atala takes a bite and dashes into the stream looking for more.

Reading from the official itinerary, one mild minder announces, schoolmarmishly, that the time has come to return to the buses.

'Oh, no, I don't think so,' Magnus says, equally mild and measured but unmoved by the need to stay on script. 'We need much more than this. Let's keep going here.' 'Here' is a rain-slicked mudslide of an incline jutting up from the path and into the dense jungly darkness above. Everyone marches after him, brushing back branches with scythes, tripods, tape recorders. Soon the camera crew has abandoned any hope of getting the shots they need and is helping Magnus pick some incandescent purple berries, the name of which nobody knows. Someone asks, through an interpreter, what he has planned for them. 'I have no idea really,' Magnus says with a smile that translates universally as: this is why we're here.

## THE RYOKAN

The middle of the night in an old and formerly serene ryokan in a sleepy coastal village south of Kanazawa. Built for a Meiji-period emperor's visit, this wood-framed room has welcomed its share of distinguished travellers over the last century or so. Never, though, have so many of the world's celebrated chefs padded across its tatami mats in their tabi toe-socks, a glittering constellation of Michelin-anointed stars gathered around the diminutive sushi bar, cinching their yukata robes with one hand, reaching out for fatty-tuna rolls with the other.

'Toro!' the chefs are shouting. This is the chefs' party the night before the gala dinner. Tomorrow the invited dignitaries will dine on their creations. Tomorrow the local media will

press them for answers about what they've learned from their four-day eating tour of Ishikawa and the broader implications for avant-garde cooking, the future of restaurants and the whole big-picture, big-think meaning of it all.

All of that can wait.

Tonight the chefs are enjoying this old ryokan, its unflappable sushi chef and each other. Tonight is about strengthening the ties that create what Alex Atala calls 'the spirit of the brigade, a brotherhood'. Tonight is about Sean Brock trying to teach René Redzepi how to speak 'Southern'.

'Fuck all y'alls!' Redzepi is saying in his best impression of a Bayou twang. Next lesson: the word 'shrimp', its syllables stretched out like taffy.

'Shreeeeeyammp,' Redzepi sings out in a credible, Danish-inflected drawl. Talk turns to varieties of sweet corn, and the Dane asks the American about the kind he uses for that famous Southern dish, grits.

'I'll show you on my arm!' Brock says. And he does, pulling up his sleeve to reveal a bright and elaborate wrist-to-shoulder tattoo of his favourite vegetables and grains.

Meanwhile, David Chang is at the bar, catching up with his mates. Unscripted, away from the cameras and the lucky invited guests, this is what Cook It Raw is all about: chefs talking shop, talking shit, sharing, relaxing into a mood of brotherly culinary cross-pollination.

The yukata-robed chef brigade that has descended on the green and beautiful Noto

157

exciting in food right now, ranging from the elemental, back-to-nature primitivism of the Nordic purists to the just-make-it-delicious borderless eclecticism of the Momofuku style. What they share, in addition to the bond of mutual respect and geeky enthusiasm, is a similarity of purpose.

Down the bar from Albert Adrià and Chang is Mauro Colagreco. The L'Arpège-trained Argentine works in the Côte d'Azur, creating vegetable-driven menus from a terraced hillside garden overlooking the Mediterranean. On the other side of the Atlantic, in Charleston, South Carolina, Sean Brock is busy conjuring the pre-Civil War culinary glory of the American South from forgotten varieties of Jimmy Red corn and heritage pigs. What connects these two, indeed what binds together the whole gang at the bar and makes them able representatives of a new breed of chef, is a common determination to move good restaurants out of the realm of the fussy, boringly tradition-bound temples of gastronomy.

Together these chefs are ramping up the ambition and tamping the pretension. 'We've been hoodwinked for so long, tricked by all these six-million-dollar kitchens with no heart and soul,' Ben Shewry says, deprecating the traditional fine-dining quest for luxury for luxury's sake. 'It's the people that make a restaurant, not the kitchen. Here we get together to talk about restaurants and cooking till the cows come home. It's more like a support group. These are very determined people who push very hard. When it comes down to it there aren't that many people who do it this way.'

'I'm actually disappointed you don't have more of a Southern accent,' Redzepi confides.

'Just give me some whiskey,' Brock responds, deadpan. 'The brain slows down.'

Japanese whisky is produced. Brock has mounted a small video camera belonging to Anthony Bourdain's TV crew on to his head, facing backwards, and is laughing his ass off. Albert Adrià is leading the wave at the sushi bar. 'Toro!' he shouts, leaping from his seat. And down the row, one by one, the cook's dream team throws its hands in the air, chanting, 'Toro! Toro!'

The prep kitchen.
Afternoon, a humming kitchen; all top chefs, no line cooks. Ben Shewry is gently washing individual leaves of foraged wasabi, brushing and counting and arranging them by size like a jeweller handling small gems. Brock is making yuzu purée for a duck dish that will never be (the traditional duck hunt with wooden nets yields no ducks). Mark Best is slicing mushrooms and figuring out how to serve his guinea fowl eggs, cooked in the wobbly-yolked onsen style, on a rectangle of Japanese cypress.

To deepen the dialogue between visiting chefs and local custom, each chef is paired with an artisan from the Utatsuyama Craft Workshop who designed the plate on which this food will be served. Mark Best drew a wooden plank, and adapted accordingly. For Redzepi there was a bright and ethereal glass base for his beautifully imagined white-on-green dessert of saké lees ice cream with a reduction of wild ginger and sorrel. Magnus Nilsson seems to have found a soulmate of quirky individuality in Nahoko Yamazaki, who created for him a lovely piece of floppy fabric. More of a primitive wall hanging than a plate, it suited Magnus fine. He named his organic assemblage of foraged mushrooms, rocks, leaves and dotted creams after one particularly apt plea that Yamazaki made during their email discussion: 'No soup, please!'

'This is the fun part,' Magnus says, wandering around the kitchen, unsure exactly what he'll do with his mushrooms and purple mystery berries. 'We travel to an amazing country with a food culture that every chef in the world is at least slightly fascinated by and we get to stay in a nice place with fun people who aren't too serious – why shouldn't it be fun? But you do work for it – you do want to make a great dish.'

Fifteen dishes, fifteen studies on the theme of nature and interpretation, the terroir of local cuisine and craftsmanship refracted through fifteen distinct viewpoints. For an idea of the range of styles this represents, consider two inspired, radically dissimilar platings: Yoshihiro Narisawa's edible candle encased in a billowy lantern of Japanese paper, and David Chang's raw hamachi served in a rustic bowl with interior ridges like a suribachi, the traditional Japanese mortar.

Taken together, these dishes offer an elegant answer to the question what is Cook It Raw? Yes, it's a brigade of chefs and excitable journalists on a culinary road trip, part sensitive cultural exchange and field study, part boys' own adventure complete with duck-trapping expeditions, cookouts and after-hours onsen (hot-spring) bonding opportunities but more than this it's an annual, evolving experiment in 'what if?' What if you convinced the best-of-class young chefs to step away from their restaurant stoves and busy normal schedules, flew them to a remote and rural setting, plied them with alcohol and coffee and encouraged them to trade ideas? What if you held a conference without panels, a culinary festival with no cooking demos or distracting autograph-seeking fans? Nothing, really, but chefs talking to other chefs in some place far from home. From these unstructured interactions, so the thinking goes, the flame of creativity might be sparked. A spark that might be carried home – like Narisawa's elegant, ephemeral lanterns carried glowing through a darkened dining room of appreciative 'ahhhs' – and fanned by experimentation until it lights the way forward to a new way of thinking about food.

The final dinner.
Evening, a glass-walled pavilion with long tables set for dinner, a window into a kitchen

within which David Chang is operating in full expletive-punctuated force. Despite a malfunctioning freezer, the general haze of jet-lag and some late and saké-fuelled nights – not to mention the friendly friction of fifteen chefs working in one unfamiliar kitchen – dinner is a shining success. Only one of Narisawa's lanterns catches fire en route to the table. The Japanese crowd applauds the spectacle. Through an interpreter Chang instructs the nattily suited and gowned crowd to get their hands dirty grating radishes and they eat it up, loving the assertive remix of familiar flavours and the DIY interactive demands of the experience.

Brock, the newcomer, manages without his ducks, bouncing back at the last minute with local pork, which he had barbecued on a wood fire outside the kitchen. 'Our boy pulled it off,' Anthony Bourdain declares. Someone else at the table quietly chants, 'USA! USA!'

The brigade, representing five continents and a fair chunk of top slots in annual best-restaurant polls, prove themselves every bit as able, agile and affable as their mountains of friendly press and rave reviews would suggest. But in a real sense, what was interesting and sort of important (if you're someone who gives thought to such peculiar concerns as the future of global high-level restaurant cooking) had already happened. It happened before the big night, away from the local press and photo-ops with invited dignitaries. The usefulness of this assembled super-league of cool dude chefs

(and it is very much a dude-ocracy) presented itself in the form of the simple luxury of relaxed, ad hoc hanging-out time, the conversations over the last few days between this clique of inventive, ambitious, influential, world-class cooks and restaurateurs.

'Dinner isn't the point,' Redzepi says. Dan Patterson adds that 'the process is the point. There's something about the energy we share. There's an energy and also a humility and a sense of humanness that's really special.'

'I think chefs are looking for this space where we can be inspired by each other,' Redzepi continues. 'Where we can visit another culture and come back with a better understanding of our own culture. An event like this is one of the few times in the year when we can do this. At most culinary events, you're up on a stage and you basically masturbate for a while.'

And it's true. The brigade avoids the mutual masturbation of back-slapping and bows. After the guests have filtered back into the night, the champagne corks are popped and talk turns to onsen baths and beer at the ryokan, to where Cook It Raw will go next year, and most pressingly, to the business of making reservations for a final lunch in Tokyo tomorrow.

Shortly after arriving in Ishikawa, the chefs will be escorted to Hosho-zushi, a local sushi restaurant. There will be a presentation of seasonal fish and a cooking demonstration followed by a meal.

A

B

A   The chefs are introduced to local seafood.

B   Dinner at Hosho-zushi, Kanazawa.

The chefs will visit Kano Shuzo saké brewery, where each chef will choose a saké to be served with their dish. Afterwards we will visit the Satoyama area to forage for mountain vegetables and indigenous herbs.

A

'I love feeling scared. It makes the whisky taste better at the end of the night.'

Sean Brock

B

A   Saké tasting at Kano Shuzo brewery.     B   Ben Shewry and Magnus Nilsson sample some saké.

C

D

E

C   The chefs plan their menu from the produce on display.

D   Sean Brock inspects the Japanese yam.

E   Seasonal produce from Ishikawa including yams, mushrooms and Japanese parsley.

F

G

F  Magnus Nilsson and Yoshihiro
Narisawa identify their finds.

G  Alex Atala scours the river bank for
wild wasabi.

H

I

J

H I  Magnus Nilsson forages in the forest.

J  The chef compare wild herbs.

N

K

L

K　Native Japanese chef Yoshihiro
　　Narisawa leads the forage.

L　René Redzepi forages for wild sorrel.

M　René Redzepi and Magnus Nilsson
　　head towards a rice paddy.

After the forage, the chefs will be served a barbecue lunch. In the afternoon they will transported to Katano Kamoike Observation Center to partake in a duck hunt using traditional Japanese nets.

A

A  Albert Adrià and Kondo Takahiko enjoy the barbecue lunch.

B

C

D

B    Sean Brock tries to catch duck for his
dish in vain.

C D    A guide shows Alex Atala how to
wield the duck-hunting net.

B

A

The chefs will enjoy dinner at the Beniya Mukayu Ryokan. The following morning the group will depart at 05:00 am for the Nanao Fish Market where they will be instructed in the ikejime technique for slaughtering fish.

A   Mistress of Beniya Mukayu Ryokan

B   Kondo Takahiko and Yoji Tokuyoshi enjoy their meal.

C   Fish buyers inspect the catch at the Nanao Fish Market.

C

D

E

C Striped jack fish, needlefish and striped grouper are among the fish on display.

D Magnus Nilsson inspects the live catch.

E The chefs watch as the ikejime technique is demonstrated.

A The chefs discuss their plans for the final dinner.

The chefs arrive at the Amadan Villa to begin preparation of their dishes for
the final meal. The meal will commence at 18:00 and will be preceded by
a cocktail reception.

A

B   The chefs enjoy a barbecue lunch prepared by Alessandro Porcelli and Andrea Petrini.

C   Alex Atala begins work preparing his dish.

D   Alexandre Gauthier plates up his dish, Earth marrow.

E   The chefs offer guidance as the freezer containing René's dish is accidentally switched to defrost.

F

G

H

F   Mark Best carefully seasons his dish.

G   Ben Shewry starts to plate up his dish into its specially made bowls.

H   Alexandre Gauthier samples Claude Bosi's dish.

I   René Redzepi starts to relax as the freezer comes back down to temperature.

Claude Bosi
Lick the monk

Mauro Colagreco
Cu + 2I —> CuI2, 2CuI2 —> 2CuI+I2

Daniel Patterson
Counter culture

Alex Atala
Jewelousy

Yoshihiro Narisawa
Inori – Prayer

Albert Adrià
Frustrated mackerel

Alexandre Gauthier
Earth marrow

Yoji Tokuyoshi
Strange fruit

Ben Shewry
Dry your eyes sweetheart

Mark Best
Norweigan wood

Magnus Nilsson
No soup, please

David Chang
Hansei

Kondo Takahiko
Polluted

Sean Brock
If pigs have wings

René Redzepi
Saké saké

### P.178 – Claude Bosi: Lick the monk

Monkfish liver, persimmon, fresh chestnuts, white turnip, ginkgo nuts, yuzu and black radish. Served as the first dish of Cook It Raw Japan's final dinner, Claude Bosi's ice cream of monkfish liver combined the subtle textures of Japanese cuisine with the more robust flavours of European cuisine.

### P.179 – Mauro Colagreco: Cu + 2I –> CuI2, 2CuI2 –> 2CuI+I2

Noto oysters, pear, ginkgo nuts, yuzu, cream and watercress. Among all the stunning plates and vessels that were crafted for the dishes, the turquoise floating island that Tomomi Ishinaga created for Mauro Colagreco might have taken first prize. The name of Colagreco's dish was a reference to a laboratory method

### P.181 – Alex Atala: Jewelousy

Ceviche of red squid, mukago yam, chilli and smoked oil. Atala's dish was one of the first of the dinner, and it showed his mastery of ceviche. Served on a crystal-clear cube of ice on top of a shiny metallic plate, small opaque cubes of red squid were coloured by pieces of chilli and dark blue mukago yams. The tiny, unpeeled yams [...]h, nutty crunch to [...]xture of the chilled [...] drops of smoked [...]dish an earthy tone [...]od.

### [Yosh]ihiro Narisawa: [...]

[...]hiitake mushrooms, [...]eboshi, dried [...]nd kombu. The [...] by the Japanese [...]risawa received the [...]able presentation [...]g. It was brought [...]'s procession, the [...]lluminated only by [...]anterns covering [...]title of the dish [...]universal prayer for [...]d nature. Around [...]dle made from a [...]burdock root filled [...]rapeseed oil lay [...]containing juicy [...]k snow crab and [...] The wrapping [...]and the candle [...]d then the dish

### P.183 – Albert Adrià: Frustrated mackerel

Sardines, mustard greens, enoki mushrooms and sofrito. Chef-wizard Albert Adrià found himself improvising his dish at the last moment. Its name derived from the fact that he couldn't get the mackerel he had planned to use. Instead he used local sardines, cut into bite size, with their beautiful silver scales on and resting in a clear aromatic broth with tiny Japanese mushrooms. The dish was served in a wooden soup bowl covered in black Urushi lacquer by Taro Oshima.

### P.184 – Alexandre Gauthier: Earth marrow

Whelks, black radish and rice crisp. Gauthier created a dish with few elements but delicious in its slightly odd, black and white appearance: lightly charred whelk slices threaded on a twig with rolled slices of black radish and a white rice crisp. It was served on a white-glazed porcelain dish with an irregular pattern of white porcelain beads of different size and shape. The visual contrasts in Gauthier's creation were mirrored by the textured contrasts between the slightly smoky, chewy whelks and the crispness of the other elements.

Albert Adrià   Alex Atala   Mark Best   Claude Bosi   Sean Brock   David Chang
Mauro Colagreco   Alexandre Gauthier   Yoshihiro Narisawa   Magnus Nilsson
Daniel Patterson   Réné Redzepi   Ben Shewry   Kondo Takahiko & Yoji Tokuyoshi

**P.185 – Yoji Tokuyoshi: Strange fruit**

Carrots, radishes, cucumber, kuritake, artichoke, coffee and rice gnocchi. Tokuyoshi and Takahiko's first dish was a fresh and beautiful creation of colour, fresh produce and textures. A chewy mochi – rice gnocchi – contrasted with the acidity of the crispy fruits and carrots, radishes, artichoke and cucumber. The round-shaped fruits and vegetables were assembled on a beautiful glass plate cut in faceted squares, the result of Eriko Asano's ambition to create the image of a dancing plate.

**P.186 – Ben Shewry: Dry your eyes sweetheart**

Shiitake broth with light soy and kelp, raw pink shrimp, fresh peanuts, shrimp roe, wild onions, chrysanthemum and wild wasabi leaves. For Shewry it was an obvious choice to work with native Japanese ingredients, paying homage to the Japanese culinary tradition. He made a broth of fresh shiitake mushrooms and poured it over raw pink shrimp, fresh peanuts, blue shrimp roe and wild onion bulbs. The dish was garnished with wild wasabi leaves picked in a creek in the Kaga mountains. Shewry named this dish in honour of his friend and fishmonger Jason Jurie, who died a few days before Cook It Raw.

**P.187 – Mark Best: Norwegian Wood**

Black cabbage, brussels sprouts, mustard greens, mushrooms, aubergine (eggplant), chestnuts, walnuts, mackerel, onsen guinea fowl egg and pine oil. In creating his dish, Mark Best was inspired by Haruki Murakami's novel Norwegian Wood and by a traditional Japanese onsen breakfast at a ryokan in Ishikawa. The dish was served on a Japanese wooden board with a feather pattern, and comprised four elements: mackerel with saké rice, mushrooms, mustard greens, and onsen guinea fowl egg in its shell with pine oil.

**P.188 – Magnus Nilsson: No soup, please**

Shimeji, Frost, Nameko, Shiba and Giant Shiitake mushrooms, oatmeal and mushroom soy, cream, lichens and wild herbs. Nilsson relied on local Japanese produce, mainly mushrooms, and on being true to his own cooking style. Foraging in the Satoyama, he picked all edible mushrooms he could find. To these he added only one ingredient he had brought with him from Sweden: his own mushroom soy, made of fermented mushroom juice and oatmeal. The nature of Nilsson's dish was dictated by the serving vessel created by Nahoko Yamazaki, which also gave it its name.

**P.189 – David Chang: Hansei**

Buri (Japanese yellowtail), turnip, kohlrabi, dried and fresh shiitake mushrooms, fermented sardines in rice bran, small green onions, konbu, yuzu and enoki. Chang's great knowledge of Japanese cuisine resulted in an dish that was partly prepared by the guests at the table. The name of the dish means self-reflection in Japanese. The specially designed bowl had serrated edges that allowed the guests to work the turnip around the edge to grate it into their dish – an interactive element that made the dish a talking point of the dinner and perhaps the most successful collaboration between a chef and artist. After grating the turnip, the diner then poured the umami-filled sauce with green onions, yuzu and enoki over it. The guests then dipped slices of lightly cured fish into the sauce by hand.

**P.190 – Kondo Takahiko: Polluted**

Okinawa spinach, island carrot, squid, whelk, sea urchin roe, black radish, Brussels sprout, cucumber, Jerusalem artichoke, sea water.

The dish, that was planned together with Massimo Bottura in Modena, was served from a boat-shaped plate made of folded paper covered in Urushi laquer. On the plate lay pieces of tree bark and dry leaves. On the right side of this was a whole Jerusalem artichoke, filled with sea urchin roe and vegetables. Before eating the stuffed crunchy shell of the tuber, the guests dipped their fingers in a small bowl of seawater, adding a taste of the sea to the dish.

**P.191 – Sean Brock: If pigs had wings**

Hay-roasted and smoked pork loin, yuzu puree, green peanuts, miso, apple, purple sweet potatoes and fresh herbs. The plate that Brock was given by Ilryul Lee had great impact on his final dish. The gray square of glazed clay was divided into four smaller squares, thus dividing the food into four elements. Then, the duck that Brock had planned to was unavailable and had to be switched to pork just a day before the dinner. Rising to these challenges, he created a dish of juicy, hay-smoked roasted pork combined with light, fresh, green and earthy flavours.

Ice cream with sake lees,
popped rice, rice crisps, sorrel
and myoga broth. Redzepi
wanted to create a mouthful
of Japanese flavours and
textures in his dessert. His main
ingredient was rice, and it came
in many forms in the beautiful
glass bowl encasing a pattern
of cracked glass: sweet sushi
rice, sake lees, rice crisps and
popped rice. The broken pieces
of white rice crisps matched
the pattern in the glass bowl
beautifully, and a broth of wild
myoga ginger and sorrel juice
from the satoyama brought
intense green colour and
flavour to the dish.

One of the things I am most proud of is the fact that I have been serving rice and beans at D.O.M since the very first day the restaurant opened. This simple combination of ingredients is one that routinely graces the dining tables and lunch pails of every laborer in Brazil. To give an idea of just how common it is, at any construction site the question asked by co-workers during a meal is 'What is the mix?', meaning 'What additional ingredients has your wife or daughter added to your dish of rice and beans?'

Though it may seem repetitive, nearly all Brazilians eat rice and beans almost every day and most of them will lament the fact that their meal is incomplete if the duo of ingredients doesn't make it onto their plate. I find it funny when I stop to think that in São Paulo – a metropolis with a population of twenty million people – the high-flying people that make up the Brazilian economic and political elite come to my restaurant to eat the same thing that the delivery boy that works for them has probably eaten for lunch.

At every lunch service it is always the same, rice and beans is one of our most requested dishes. This is because the dish is a tradition, it is part of what makes up the Brazilian cultural identity and transcends the imaginary boundaries of wealth and social status. It is with a genuine sense of joy that I watch people enjoy my rice and beans. It is proof that I'm on the right path. After all, in Italy, when a mother cooks, everybody gathers around the table, but when a grandmother cooks, transmitting all of her years of understanding and experience into her dishes, then it's a real celebration. A French chef is labeled as a maestro when he prepares amazing French food, but this is the food that he has been eating and cooking since he was a child. So, to be a great Brazilian cook you must be able to prepare delicious rice and beans.

The difference between what is good, very good and exceptional can be found in repetition. A chef must master the basics before he can create something that is truly exceptional, and the only way to master something is to repeat the process many times, honing your skills and making slight changes to your methods until you have reached your own version of perfection. Creative cuisine is not about creating illusions and it's not about inventing something that is brand new, in fact, it's the opposite. The path to truly great cooking lies in recognizing what has come before; looking at classic recipes, flavour combinations and techniques and pushing them that little bit further. Creativity is not only invention. Creativity is not only looking ahead. Creativity is ultimately doing something that you already know, but in an unusual and surprising way.

This is the reasoning that I have founded my cuisine on, finding unusual and forgotten ingredients that are native to Brazil and fusing them with traditional classical techniques to create something 'new'. This tendency of looking back in order to go forward is something I have always been aware of in my own cooking, but it was not until my trip to Ishikawa, Japan, for Cook It Raw that I understood just how important tradition is in the search for culinary perfection. It was the fourth edition of Cook It Raw and everybody was buzzing with excitement and expectation. We had all been through some amazing experiences at the previous Cook It Raw events, each one had both positive and negative sides, which kept our memories fresh and enhanced the spirit of the events. Each one had been a truly raw experience.

The beauty of Cook It Raw lies in the fact that by presenting us chefs with these challenges, reducing the ingredients available to us, taking us out of our comfort zones and stripping away our egos there is a real chance of failure. With the chance of failure comes fear, and it is this fear that really gets our collective creative juices flowing. The idea of Cook It Raw is to embrace an unfamiliar location, immerse yourself in its produce, culture and traditions and then interpret that location through food – this does not always mean that you get a

great recipe at the end, but the journey is always exciting.

Japan inhabits the dreams of every cook. It's a place where the millenary art of cooking teaches that simplicity and the quest for purity should be the fundamental goal in the kitchen and that to reach this purity a cook requires balance, precision and concentration. The country was still reeling from the catastrophic earthquake and tsunami that had hit earlier in the year, but that didn't temper the enthusiastic hospitality and heartfelt sense of welcome that were extended to us throughout our stay. Everywhere we went, we were welcomed with a genuine smile and we soon learnt that this friendly and generous reception was intrinsic to the Japanese character. It was this hospitality that made our trip so special, though there were many unforgettable moments: walking around the bright lights of Tokyo, exploring Ishikawa, foraging for herbs and fruits in the woods and seeing wild wasabi growing on a riverbed for the first time to name a few.

And then there were the meals. With every meal we better understood what lay at the root of Japanese food culture. The best ingredients, simply prepared with enormous skill. The ingredients weren't over seasoned or masked by heavy sauces. The ingredients were allowed to sing. Our dishes had to do so too.

Ishikawa is a unique place that is steeped in tradition. It is especially famous for its local craft and lacquerware and I will always remember the moment that a local artist presented me with the beautiful plate that had been specially made for me and would inspire the dish I was going to make. Constructed from metal, elegantly curved and precise, it reminded me immediately of a jewellery box and the perfect recipe came to mind; I remembered the tapiocas of my native Brazil, which shimmer like beautiful pearls and would decorate the dish to perfection. Then I thought of how jealous a gnarled oyster would be of these simple, elegant orbs. The duo was formed: oysters and tapioca. Even the name of the dish had implanted itself into my mind: 'Jewelousy', a combination of the words 'jewel' and 'jealousy'. So perfect that I thought I was done, but at an event like Cook It Raw the capacity for failure is always there and you have to be adaptable to succeed. By forming such a clear idea of what I wanted to make so early, I had almost certainly set myself up to fail.

The final dinner was about to begin and I had succeeded in destroying everything that I had made the day before. I didn't have any idea of how to salvage my dish so I swallowed my pride and asked my fellow chefs for help. The kitchen was flared up with the spirit of the event: a bunch of chefs constantly improvising and adapting, creating and learning as they go. Every chef was consulting with the others, sharing ideas, overcoming doubts and offering advice. This is one of the key features of Cook It Raw, this is what keeps us going back. Professional chefs are traditionally fiercely competitive, secretive of their recipes and

techniques and jealous of others. Not so with us, we have become a brotherhood.

It was while exchanging ideas with the other chefs that I realized that no one had made use of one of Japan's freshest and best-quality ingredients in their dish: the squid. We had all overlooked the poor, neglected squid and it was now the only chance to save my dish. Driven by both inspiration and a sense of panic, I quickly marinated the squid in coal oil and set it aside. I then asked chef Narisawa, himself native to Japan, if he could help me to source some blocks of ice. A few hours later I was presented with a beautiful stack of ice blocks, each one translucent, perfect and identical. I quickly assembled my finely chopped red squid with coal oil. The fresh squid texture and appearance was perfect. I matched the squid with tiny Mukago yams, typical to the region of Ishikawa, which I had found during our foraging fieldtrip to the woods a few days earlier. Against all odds and at the last minute, I had managed to turn the difficulty in simplicity.

But it was after recording a TV program with some chefs for the NHK Chanel that I learnt the greatest lesson. We had all been tired before we arrived at the TV station and the filming had taken much longer than we had expected. After it was complete, there was a tension in the air but we were all invited to enjoy one last meal at a sushi restaurant. Everybody was tired and strung out and would much rather have returned to the hotel and rest, but Japan and its people had been so kind and accommodating that it seemed cruel to turn down such a generous invitation. I thought for a second, took a deep breath and, against everything my tired bones were telling me, said 'I will go!' The others immediately joined me. 'If one goes, everybody goes!' they said. Such is the spirit of Cook It Raw.

We were separated into small, weary groups and ferried to UMI, a legendary sushi ya in Tokyo. As ever, we were welcomed with the by now familiar Japanese smile at the restaurant. When I arrived, Albert Adrià and René Redzepi were already settled and smiling. I joined them and we sat timidly, watching the highly skilled chef open his fridge and start to prepare his delicacies. As if by magic, the fatigue and hostility that had been gradually building melted away to be replaced once more with joy and fellowship.

We all sat mesmerized as the chef began to assemble dish after dish of remarkable sushi. Though the food looked beautifully simple on the plate, the care the chef was taking with his ingredients, the mastery of his knife techniques and the decisiveness of his cuts all revealed that we were watching a true master at work. Each dish was beautifully presented and allowed each ingredient to stand out individually, with all of the individual flavours coming together to form a magnificent whole.

The incredible skill and good humour of the sushi chef was infectious, and our collective spirits were raised ever higher as each new and amazing dish emerged. The sushi chef was teaching us as he cooked. We were all fascinated by his mastery of the art, and the mood was further buoyed by the joy that only exceptional food can bring. The sushi master's mood reflected our own, and he did not hide his satisfaction in the pleasure his food was giving us.

At that moment I understood why the Japanese revere a sushi master so highly. To serve a dish to people who have been eating it their entire life and still amaze and surprise them with your skill and lightness of touch is truly an art. It is important to first master the classic dishes, know the traditional recipes and learn how to balance ingredients perfectly before you can try and create something new. I knew that I would never be able to make sushi as well as this chef. He had grown up with the tradition, the dedication and the passion needed to make perfect sushi. These dishes of raw fish, perfect in their simplicity and unsurpassed in their skill were his life's work.

This remarkable sushi was like my own rice and beans, and our chef had dedicated his life to it. Tradition then, is at the root of great cooking. Improvisation, flair and creativity are all vital, and moments of inspiration do come along. But without a basis of classical technique and an understanding of ingredients and flavours that you can only achieve through diligence and study, it is impossible to go from good to great. This applies to all artforms, not just cooking. A writer or a painter can have great flair and originality, but without some classical training and without an understanding of the rules it becomes very hard to break them. To be the best at something you need to look backwards first, and it was the centenary, delicate, precise and poignant tradition of Japan that taught me this. A toast to it!

# Cook It Raw: Conclusion

THE DINNERS:

[I]         Denmark
          N A T U R E
       Zero energy cooking

Cook It Raw's inaugural dinner in
Copenhagen sees the chefs explore
nature through a zero energy cooking
challenge.


[II]         Italy
        C R E A T I V I T Y
       Chef versus winter

During the depths of a Collio winter
Cook It Raw's chefs prepare dinner
in an experiment of creativity.

[III]         Finland
       C O L L A B O R A T I O N
        Cooking in the wild

Cook It Raw heads into the Lappish
wilds to test the strength of the
brotherhood by holding a collaborative
dinner.


[IV]          Japan
           F U T U R E
      Avant-garde meets tradition

The chefs meet the producers and crafts
men of Ishikawa to create a Cook It Raw
dinner that marries avant-garde cooking
with tradition.


THE PRINCIPLES:

[I]  Nature rules
[II] Limitations boost creativity

[III] Collaboration not competition
[IV] Look back to look forward


THE CHEFS:

| | | |
|---|---|---|
| ✗ | Albert Adrià | ES |
| ✗ | Iñaki Aizpitarte | FR |
| ✗ | Alex Atala | BR |
| ✗ | Fredrik Andersson | SE |
| ✗ | Pascal Barbot | FR |
| ✗ | Mark Best | AU |
| ✗ | Claude Bosi | UK |
| ✗ | Massimo Bottura | IT |
| ✗ | Sean Brock | US |
| ✗ | David Chang | US |
| ✗ | Mauro Colagreco | AR |
| ✗ | Quique Dacosta | ES |
| ✗ | Alexandre Gauthier | FR |

| | | |
|---|---|---|
| ✗ | Ichiro Kubota | JP |
| ✗ | Yoshihiro Narisawa | JP |
| ✗ | Magnus Nilsson | SE |
| ✗ | Petter Nilsson | SE |
| ✗ | Daniel Patterson | US |
| ✗ | René Redzepi | DK |
| ✗ | Davide Scabin | IT |
| ✗ | Ben Shewry | XX |
| ✗ | Kondo Takahiko | JP |
| ✗ | Yoji Tokuyoshi | JP |
| ✗ | Hans Välimäki | FI |
| ✗ | Joachim Wissler | DE |

# Cook It Raw and the Future – by Alessandro Porcelli

In all honesty, when I first started Cook It Raw back in 2009, I wasn't really aware of exactly what I was creating or indeed what it would eventually become. What I did know though was that I had a definite opportunity – the United Nations Climate Conference – and strong motivation – a growing weariness amongst the food community with traditional chefs conference – to make something happen. In hindsight however, these two things by themselves were not enough. The real impetus – the difference between Raw being just an another idea and its actual realisation – was good, old-fashioned guts. Once the inspiration behind Raw had struck me, with René and Andrea's help, I just did it.

Since its inception, this enterprising, gung-ho determination has always been one of the greatest drivers of Raw. None of the delicious events, which you've seen explained in detail throughout the chapters of this book, were ever easy. No. Each had to be dragged into reality, kicking and screaming.

After four editions, I am totally convinced that all the work and struggle that has gone into creating and continuing Cook It Raw has been worth it. We – the chefs, the local people we have met, me myself – we have all learned so much from every episode and the Raw experience in its entirety. In Copenhagen, during our very first endevour, we challenged climate change. Dishes made were stark statements about the future health of the planet and, having picked and plucked most of the ingredients ourselves, we had renewed appreciation for our natural surroundings. Returning for a second installment, this time in Collio, our chefs were pitted against the harsh Italian winter. Faced with a natural larder that was bare, they were forced to rely on their own resources. Their creativity didn't let them down. Our adventure in Lapland taught us a lesson about surviving in extreme conditions: you need to collaborate. Finally, in Japan, we were gently reminded that there will always be a place for tradition in the kitchen and that often, in order to move forward, we must look back.

What, if anything, has Cook It Raw and its four meetings actually accomplished?

Bringing together such a unique group of smart, skilled people is not easy; being able to create a place where they feel comfortable and perform at their best is even harder. However, even before that first meeting, I knew this would be essential if Raw was to achieve anything. The chefs needed somewhere they could enjoy themselves and relax. It was only afterwards that we realized that Raw could be more, that it could also be somewhere that the chefs felt safe to fail.

Taking risks and making mistakes is how we move forward – this is true in every profession. However, chefs like René, David and Massimo, to name just a few, are under such constant scrutiny – every other plate leaving the pass will be critiqued by some guidebook, journalist or blogger – that they were losing the safety to play with their ideas without unforgiving judgment. Between Copenhagen and Japan, Raw has created a community of friendship and trust and this community has become such a haven for these guys.

However, this is just one result of Raw – and if the impact of this event were limited only to those who attended it, I would feel as if I missed a chance to make a difference, however big or small.

Thankfully, I do not believe that this has been the case. I am certain that Raw has been a positive force for change both in those societies that we have visited as well as in the wider food trade. I have seen it myself. First, capitalising on the position that chefs today occupy in the public eye and the attention that their actions now attract, we were able to shine a powerful spotlight on Raw's destinations. This has led to a benefit to local producers and residents, bringing them onto the world scene as well as actually bringing neighbours together – people who though actually living nearby to each other, would not have met were it not for Raw. Cases of both of these are many, but one especially nice one includes Josko Sirk, the owner of restaurant La Subida. He hosted us at the second Raw in Collio and made a terrific impression on everyone there. Off the back of the event, he was invited to present at Identita Golose – Italy's biggest food event.

Beyond this, Raw has provided a way to understand larger food issues better. Food became the medium and local terroir the lens through which some of the greatest global environmental problems became real and tangible rather than simply headlines in the newspaper. The trickle down effect is inevitable.

Cook It Raw's success and, even more so, the concrete consequences of this entire project have far exceeded my expectations. A major factor responsible for this is the amazing chemistry between those in the group – it is a wonderful experience being able to work with people who are literally the best in the world at what they do as well as close friends.

Upon reflection, I am left considering what is the legacy left behind by Cook It Raw?

Yes, there are the friendships that have been forged, the community that has been built, but there's another answer, one a little romantic actually. For me, Cook It Raw is proof that if you really believe in something, work hard at it and refuse to give up, then anything is possible – even for a crazy Italian, like me.

'I was thinking of preparing a… Canard à la ficelle'

At 11.30 am on a scorching August 21st, Iñaki Aizpitarte managed to focus his thoughts via multiple shots of caffeine. As the coffee worked its magic and the cobwebs were swept aside, his thoughts turned unintentionally, almost against his free will, fitting in the slacks of the visionary pothead.

'This summer I was on holiday in Andalusia with my son Diego. For sure, emails were not on my mind. The next Cook It Raw neither.

Back in Paris, I found out that Redzepi wanted to gig with wild berries, Patterson longed for lake fish and Magnus thought of chopping down a pine tree and using its sap to make a sorbet. I told myself then that: "What the fuck! Trying to do a canard à la ficelle could not be a much crazier idea than theirs".'

The shambolic Chevalier des Arts et des Lettres (also recently knighted neo-Maître Rôtisseur de France) had, once more, almost inadvertently, seized to the letter and much better than many others, the true spirit of Raw.

Less is more. Let's make it clear, once and for all: the less you do, the better it is. Canard à la ficelle, a duck tied to a string and slowly cooked for hours using the residual heat from the flames. A well-thought dish, an objet trouvé, an authorless creation, free at last of messianic messages. An instant creation, an almost aleatory one at the mercy of everyone passing by. Offered to the posse of chefs hanging around. Let's give it a push, let's turn it around. Let's spin it around on its string, the thighs or the back (not so) close to the chimney heat. Wait a little now, let's check it out all together – but en passant – while sweating like pigs and gulping down a couple of beers just in front of the flames to see what effect it made.

Hey guys, next time you stumble into Iñaki, please tell him that, once upon a time, many many years ago, more than thirty, when he was a streetwise kid in knickerbockers, a hugely gifted British guitar hero, Fred Frith, with thick sideburns and a glorious mane, would play his guitar on his lap. Its grip laid bare like a sacrilegious keyboard, he would insert strings, screws, matches, pebbles and bolts – just to find out what effect it made (Solo Guitar, Fred Frith – Recommended Records 1974).

Although they have never met, Fred and Iñaki are quite alike. One of them plays music and the other cooks, but both are constantly experimenting, just to see what the final results will be. Both of them looking for those moments of perfect alchemy discovered by pure chance. In many ways they are a bit like Nietzsche who, as everybody knows, liked to philosophise while walking. Forager ante litteram, old pal Nietzsche made his best discoveries the day he stopped searching.

O Almighty God, save Cook It Raw from enslaving its soul. Take the burden from its shoulders, deliver it from the misery of the world, break its chains and free it from the need to preach. The true spirit of Raw is not found in the collaboration of star chefs, but in that of a strongly bonded, almost incestuous family. Never forget, the family that lays together, stays together.

Each event sees the Raw brotherhood, like the members of Tolkien's Fellowship of the Ring, set off into the unknown, free of GPS or golden parachutes. If Tolkien were still alive he would surely be petting our Hobbits (like others would stroke young chicks) as they escape from the cages of their kitchens and burst forth into the wilds in search of adventure. Being a Baggins is a truly great profession! He might have longer hair and a beard on his once clean-shaven face, but when Redzep(pelin) sets off on his rural quest he has a look of edgy curiosity in his eyes and an unrelenting desire to touch everyone and everything, to connect the most intimate with the universal. He's not alone in his walking and thinking. He proceeds with his fellow pilgrims through the long and winding road, far away from the brain administrators and the bureaucrats of legitimate sensations. Every footstep should be a thought, every night around the campfire an opportunity to seed and plant. Ideas and concepts, of course. As Joseph Beuys and Massimo Bottura, our dearest Gianni & Pinotto, remind us: 'We should never stop planting.'

Interior – daylight. The stage: the well-mannered sitting room of a polite couple of farmers, in a far away country. It's cosy inside, while outside the village is soaked by the universal flood.

Question: 'Why is that portrait of that elegant gentleman hanging upside down?'
Answer: 'In this part of the world, it's an old custom, respected in every household, to turn the portrait of an old Jew upside down. The richer and more powerful the individual concerned, the more it is thought that the picture will ensure health, prosperity and happiness for the family.'

May Cook It Raw then fall into the shoes of the ever Wandering Jew, without a roof to call its own but welcome everywhere. Cautious and circumspect under the leaden sky. The roads are tree-lined, but in order to travel lightly, off the beaten track, slipping past the gatekeepers of thought, it's necessary to cross hills, climb mountains and navigate rivers in full flow. Beware of the backwash of the sixth sense, of smooth plains, when the path seems free of any dangers. It will be then that the Siren of Ease will link arms with exhaustion.

Amon Tobin, the globetrotting Brazilian musician, cautions: 'Keep your distance' (Foley Room, Ninja Tune Records, 2007). He knows quite well the perils of getting too close, too comfortable. He knows that without distance and a little dose of the unknown there's no perspective, no point of view. And so it is at Raw. It is by learning to fall – all together – that we discover how to rise again. 'Let's fail together' urged Redzep(pelin) some time ago, as he welcomed new recruits to the Raw fraternity. And never was a motto more appealing. To make mistakes and then to mend one's ways. To draw lessons from experience. To follow the mood and the idea of the moment. To see it take shape and be embraced by all.

A wild bunch of wandering, rootless cosmopolitans, Cook It Raw is not just a group: it is an individual journey. An introspective leap, a session of seminal refocusing. It is a thousand leagues from athletic contests or competitions. The chefs start off scattered to better lose themselves. Some will come and go, some will rest and some will sharpen their weapons. There will always be braggarts, but the false humanism of the smartass is just an attempt to get a cover story. We should be wary of shamans who go arm-in-arm with merchants to the temple.

We gather at night in monastic cells. Everyone in his own sphere, in his own little mononuclear habitat, ideal for circumscribing his limits and possibilities. A tiny space that is cut to measure, where we can take a fresh look at ourselves. A space where we can explore intuitions and premonitions without ever fearing the riffs of repetition and difference or the shadow of defeat. An oasis that is closed but still open to the winds, to the intoxication of starting from scratch. A free zone where we can abandon the dead weight of prejudice. Raw supplements the space of the most profound 'me', alone and beautiful but with the whole world in the room. To each his own. A spiritual exercise made to measure.

The copyright to this exercise is not ours, of course, but belongs to an ancient sage, Saint Ignatius Loyola. He was no pleasure seeker, but an aesthete little accustomed to fatuous social mores, who, in the solitude of his cell, dug out his own approach to spirituality. He went further, putting his own faith into play, intoning vows and chants, thoughts and fears. He made himself an object of abstinence. Elevation through prayer and through language. Love, devotion and surrender. A work of personal constriction, a chastity belt, a meditative piece of introspection. Less is more, poverty is the real richness.

So, forget the Magimix. Even in the most luxurious lodge resort, leave your ego and certainties in the cupboard. Cook the way you think with the few elements picked up or dreamt during the night. Strive to reach new knowledge and enjoy the fortuitous glow of an idea snatched in passing, caught by chance. Raw is a spiritual exercise to catch sight of our other selves, to reach beyond ourselves. Picking up thoughts growing here and there like wild mushrooms in a dark forest. To look for those mushrooms that spring up between shade and light, forests and hills, fissures and steep crags, you must go at the pace of the unexpected, exercise and indulge your curiosity. Canard à la ficelle for everyone!

Born (already!) a century ago, the American composer John Cage, who was no fool, would not only eat his mushrooms, but percussively play with them as natural metaphors and real instruments. Cage collected mushrooms even more than the wisest man of Earth, Milarepa the anchorite. So take note of these two, Cage and Saint Ignatius Loyola, a fine pair of buddy-buddies. Bouncers on the door be aware, Johnny and Ignatius are two real VIPs to put on the next Cook It Raw guest list!

Acknowledgements:
I would like to thank all of the chefs who participated in the gatherings, in particular my dearest friend René Redzepi who has given me his support since day one.

My deepest gratitude goes to Andrea Petrini with whom I have shared many memorable moments in the perilous attempts to make Cook It Raw happen.

My sincere appreciation goes to Carla Capalbo for helping out in Collio and for introducing me to some of the most incredible people in the area – Marco Perco, Josko Sirk and family and Edi Keber – without their generosity Cook It Raw Collio would not have been so beautifully intense.

For the Lappish experience, I owe much gratitude to Timo Nieminen and the Hullu Poro crowd, without them no reindeer would have been slaughtered for the Raw cause. I would also like to thank Kenneth Nars for introducing me to the people that helped make Cook It Raw Lapland so special.

My gratitude goes also to Tarek Abbar, Gourmanity and chef Narisawa-san for making Cook It Raw Japan happen.

A huge thanks goes to my friend Ali Kurshat Altinsoy, for helping me to put my thoughts in order and getting them down on paper. Finally, thank you to my family for helping me to realize my dream.
Alessandro Porcelli

The Publisher would like to thank all of the chefs, writers and photographers who have contributed to the book; and Melanie Hibbert, Sophie Hodgkin, Esther Jagger and Margot Levy for their hard work on the project.

Picture credits: b = bottom, l = left, m = middle, r =right, t = top
Per-Anders Jorgensen – jacket front flap tr, jacket front tl, jacket front tml, jacket front tmr, jacket front bl, jacket back tml, jacket back bmr, 13r, 15l, 19r, 21r, 24r, 33–56, 73–96; Erik Olsson – jacket front flap br, jacket front bml, jacket front br, jacket back tmr, jacket back bml, jacket back bl, jacket back flap t, 15r, 17l, 18l, 19l, 20r, 23, 161–192; Erik Refner – jacket front tr, jacket front bmr, jacket back tr, jacket back tl, jacket back flap b, 16l, 20l, 113–144; Anton Sucksdorff – 13l, 14, 16l, 17r, 18r, 21l, 22, 24l.

Phaidon Press Limited
Regent's Wharf
All Saints Street
London N1 9PA

Phaidon Press Inc.
180 Varick Street
New York, NY 10014

First published 2013
© 2013 Phaidon Press Limited

ISBN 978 0 7148 6549 2

A CIP catalogue record for this book is available from the British Library.

Commissioning Editor: Emilia Terragni
Project Editors: Daniel Hurst and Emma Robertson
Production Controller: Vanessa Todd-Holmes

Designed by Matthew Fenton and Haakon Spencer